SHAKESPEARE

THE MERCHANT OF VENICE IN EVERYDAY ENGLISH

COLES EDITORIAL BOARD

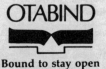

Bound to stay open

Publisher's Note

Otabind (Ota-bind). This book has been bound using the patented Otabind process. You can open this book at any page, gently run your finger down the spine, and the pages will lie flat.

ABOUT COLES NOTES

COLES NOTES have been an indispensible aid to students on five continents since 1948.

COLES NOTES are available for a wide range of individual literary works. Clear, concise explanations and insights are provided along with interesting interpretations and evaluations.

Proper use of COLES NOTES will allow the student to pay greater attention to lectures and spend less time taking notes. This will result in a broader understanding of the work being studied and will free the student for increased participation in discussions.

COLES NOTES are an invaluable aid for review and exam preparation as well as an invitation to explore different interpretive paths.

COLES NOTES are written by experts in their fields. It should be noted that any literary judgement expressed herein is just that — the judgement of one school of thought. Interpretations that diverge from, or totally disagree with any criticism may be equally valid.

COLES NOTES are designed to supplement the text and are not intended as a substitute for reading the text itself. Use of the NOTES will serve not only to clarify the work being studied, but should enhance the reader's enjoyment of the topic.

ISBN 0-7740-2987-0

© COPYRIGHT 1993 AND PUBLISHED BY
COLES PUBLISHING COMPANY
TORONTO—CANADA
PRINTED IN CANADA

Manufactured by Webcom Limited
Cover finish: Webcom's Exclusive **Duracoat**

CHARACTERS IN THE PLAY

The Duke of Venice
The Prince of Morocco }
The Prince of Arragon }   Suitors of Portia.
Antonio: A merchant.
Bassanio: Antonio's friend; suitor of Portia.
Gratiano }
Salerio }   Friends of Antonio and Bassanio.
Solanio }
Lorenzo: A young man in love with Jessica.
Shylock: A Jewish moneylender.
Tubal: A Jew; Shylock's friend.
Launcelot Gobbo: A clown; servant of Shylock.
Old Gobbo: Father of Launcelot.
Leonardo: Servant of Bassanio.
Balthasar }
Stephano }   Servants of Portia.
Portia: An heiress.
Nerissa: Portia's lady-in-waiting.
Jessica: Daughter of Shylock.
Nobles of Venice, court officers, jailer, servants and attendants.

[Setting: Venice and Belmont.]

ACT I • SCENE 1

[A street in Venice.]
[Enter Antonio, Salerio and Solanio.]

Antonio: To tell the truth, I am at a loss to explain this feeling of sadness that has seized me. It is quite as depressing to me as you tell me its effect is upon you. I am in complete ignorance of its cause, and why it should seize upon me I do not yet know. Indeed, I scarcely recognize myself, so foolishly have I been overcome by this feeling of depression.

Salerio: Your thoughts are troubled as they fly over the seas, following the fortunes of your richly laden vessels. With swelling sails and stately motion, they glide along like the ships in the citizens' processions. Like great lords or wealthy merchants passing the poorer citizens in the street, your tall vessels with their widespread sails sweep past the smaller trading ships. These smaller ships dip and bend to them on the waves, as if offering respect to those higher than themselves.

Solanio: Indeed, I assure you that, if I were engaged in such traffic and had to risk my hopes of success upon the waters in that way, the subject would certainly occupy the greater part of my thoughts. I would be forever throwing up blades of grass to see whether the breeze was against my ships or favorable to them. I would continually be studying maps and pondering over charts, looking for safe harbors for my vessels. And, most certainly, I would feel depressed whenever anything seemed likely to turn out unfavorably toward my enterprise.

Salerio: Even when I blew my breath upon my food to cool it, I would suddenly be seized with chilly fear, for it would suggest to me the terrible injury a strong gale at sea might do to my ships. And every time I saw the sand running out of the hourglass, it would bring before my mind a picture of sandbanks and shoals. I would picture my rich vessel ashore on a sandbank and see it gradually sink and heel over, until at last, with her masts dipped low until they lay on the sand, and her sides stood out above them, she bent and touched the ground in which she would find a grave.

If I went to church, the stones of the sacred building would immediately suggest to me the rocks that, with one

1

touch, could split my ship's wooden sides, strewing the waves with the precious spices of cargo, and clothing them in floating silks, with which my vessels had been laden. At one moment her freight would be priceless. The moment after, all my wealth would have vanished. And, if I pictured all this in my mind, is it surprising that I would also be able to picture the effect of my losses and feel sorrowful in consequence? No, you need not argue the matter. It is Antonio's anxiety for his vessels that is depressing him.

Antonio: You are mistaken, I assure you. I am thankful to say that all my hopes do not depend upon one enterprise, nor have I risked the whole of my wealth in one scheme only. Even should I have some losses this year, I will not be entirely ruined, so that it is not my commercial concerns that are causing my unhappiness.

Salerio: Then it must be love that is making you so pensive.

Antonio: Nonsense!

Salerio: Is that not the cause either? Then the only thing one can say is that you are unhappy because you are not happy. You might just as well begin to play jokes and give as your reason that you were happy because you were not unhappy. But really, when one comes to think of it, by the image of Janus, which looks both ways, there are some curious creatures in the world. Some have merry natures and are continually laughing, whether the things they see are subjects for mirth or not. Others, with sourest expression, will not even open their lips to laugh at anything, though the most serious old warrior were to swear that the joke was most amusing.

[Enter Bassanio, Lorenzo and Gratiano.]

Solanio: I see your worthy relative, Bassanio, approaching with Gratiano and Lorenzo, so I will now leave. You will now have more pleasing companionship than ours.

Salerio: If these better friends had not appeared, I would not have left you until I had cheered you up, and seen you in better spirits.

Antonio: I appreciate your kindness and respect you greatly. I am sure you must have affairs of your own that need your attention, so take this opportunity of leaving me in good hands.

Salerio: Good morning, worthy signiors.

Bassanio: My two good friends, please tell me when we shall be able to meet and spend a merry hour together. We seldom meet now. In truth, we are almost strangers to each other. Can we not remedy this? Can we not see one another more often?

Salerio: We will make a point of being at liberty when you are, Bassanio.

[Exit Salerio and Solanio.]

Lorenzo: Since you have found Antonio, signior Bassanio, Gratiano and I need not stay. But please do not forget where we are to dine together.

Bassanio: I shall certainly be there.

Gratiano: Signior Antonio, you look ill. Indeed, you are greatly altered. I fear you give too much thought to worldly affairs and the cares of business. I assure you, sir, that those who allow themselves to be worried by business cares do not enjoy the good of their prosperity.

Antonio: Nay, I keep the world and its concerns in their proper place, Gratiano. I merely look upon it as a passing drama in which everyone has been assigned a certain character. I have not been cast for a cheerful part, that is all.

Gratiano: Well, I would rather have the jester's part, myself. If I am to have wrinkles, let them be caused by laughter instead of old age. I would rather have the hot-blooded fire of youth, fed with wine, than the dull deadness of a heart grown cold. I never could see any reason why a living man, full of the vigor of manhood, should repress his spirits and force himself to stillness, until he looks like a marble image of his grandfather. Nor could I see why he should be as quiet and unemotional when he is awake as if he were still asleep, until he gradually becomes jaundiced through sheer melancholy. I assure you, Antonio (and, believe me, I am speaking in this manner only because I wish you well), I have seen a certain type of people who restrain every emotion and repress every show of feeling in order that their faces may be always grave, solemn and sedate. They are afraid even to speak, in case it would disturb the solemnity of their expressions. By this means, they try to obtain a reputation for the deepest wisdom. They wish to create an

3

impression that they, and they alone, possess words of wisdom, and, aside from them, none other is worthy to open his lips.

My dear Antonio, people like these are only considered wise as long as they do not speak. As soon as they begin to talk, they speak such nonsense that those who hear them are almost certain to call their brother a fool. But I have no time to go into the subject just now. Only do not, Antonio, be one of those who seek, by their grave and melancholy looks, to acquire a reputation for wisdom. We must go, Lorenzo. I will leave you, sirs, for the present, and finish my little sermon after we have dined.

Lorenzo: Farewell, then, until we meet at dinner. I am becoming like those wise folk that Gratiano tells of, who never speak. When I am in his company, I never get a chance to open my lips.

Gratiano: If you are my companion for a year or two longer, I promise you, you will forget what your own voice sounds like.

Antonio: Adieu, my friend. I think, after all your good advice, I must try to become more talkative.

Gratiano: That is very good of you, in truth. Indeed, the only tongue that should not be heard to speak is an ox tongue, dried.

[Exit Gratiano and Lorenzo.]

Antonio: What is one to think of all that, now?

Bassanio: Oh! Gratiano can pour out an endless stream of talk on the flimsiest subjects better than anyone else I know. If you try to find the point of his speeches, it is like hunting for two grains of good grain in an immense quantity of chaff. It takes a tremendous time to find them, and then they are not sufficient to repay you for your trouble.

Antonio: Now, keep your promise to tell me who the lady is to whom you vowed you would pay your devotions.

Bassanio: I know that you are aware, Antonio, how greatly I have injured my fortunes by keeping up a more showy style of living than my moderate income could support for any length of time. Even now I am not complaining that I can no longer live in such a luxurious style. I am more concerned as to how I am to be able to repay, honestly, the heavy debts I have incurred already, by my great extravagance. You, Antonio, have given me the most, both in coin and in friendship and affection. Your affection gives me a guarantee that I may unfold to you all the plans and schemes I have been arranging to pay my creditors and feel that I am no longer in debt.

Antonio: Certainly, my dear Bassanio, tell me all. If your project is, as you yourself always are, honorable, then I promise you that everything I have, money, influence or personal help, is entirely at your service.

Bassanio: When I was a boy at school and went shooting, if I lost one of my arrows, I took another exactly like it and shot it in the same direction, watching it more carefully than the first. By thus risking the second, I was often able to regain both. I am giving you this example of what I did in boyish days because my plan is just as innocent and open. I am deeply in your debt already, and I fear that, like other reckless youths, I am unable to repay you. But, if you agree to send more money in the same direction as the former sums, I will so carefully watch the expenditure of it that I have good hope of either regaining all, or, at least, being able to repay the sum you risk. I will also gratefully acknowledge my obligation to you for your former loans.

Antonio: You are well enough acquainted with me, Bassanio, to know that you need not waste time with all this roundabout appeal to my affection for you. In fact, I look upon it as a greater injury to me that you would seem to doubt that I would willingly give you my last penny than the possibility that you would actually spend all my wealth. Point out to me how I can help you, and the help shall be forthcoming. I only wait to learn.

Bassanio: Living at Belmont is a lady who has had great wealth left to her. She has also great beauty, but, better still than mere beauty, she is possessed of many virtues. In former times, she has sent glances in my direction, which I interpreted as wordless messages to me. She is called Portia and in every respect is the equal of that Portia who was the wife of Brutus and daughter of Cato. Her fame has spread far and wide. From every part of the globe, famous and valiant suitors come seeking her hand in marriage. Her shining hair adorns her pretty head like the golden fleece that Jason went to seek. Her home at Belmont is turned into a modern land of Colchis, to which many a Jason comes to seek and win that golden head for himself. Dear Antonio, if I were only rich enough to present myself among them, I feel so sure of success that I do not doubt I would be happy enough to win her.

Antonio: My wealth, as you know, is contained in my ships at sea. At this moment, I have nothing in hand, of either coin or goods, that I could give to you at once. But, go to the merchants and see what can be raised on the security of my name. I will stretch my credit as far as it will reach to supply you with what is necessary to go wooing the lovely Portia at Belmont. Let us both make inquiries immediately as to who can lend us the money. I have not the slightest doubt that I shall be able to obtain it, either on the security of my name, or from feelings of personal friendship.

[Exit.]

ACT I • SCENE 2

[Belmont. A room in Portia's house.]
[Enter Portia and Nerissa.]

Portia: Truly, Nerissa, this immense universe is too much for my small frame. I am tired of it.

Nerissa: Dear lady, you might reasonably say so if you were as unfortunate in it as you are fortunate. And, yet, I do not know. As far as I have observed, the people who have too much are as troubled and worried as those who have too little. It is more than moderate good fortune, therefore, to be comfortably placed in the medium state between need and overabundance. They who have an overabundance of good things worry themselves sooner into the appearance of old age, but they who have merely a comfortable living enjoy life much longer.

Portia: Very worthy proverbs, and intelligently delivered.

Nerissa: If they were acted upon, they would be worthier still.

Portia: If it were as easy to act upon good advice as it is to know what is good, everything in the world would be much better and further advanced than it is now. The preacher who puts into practice what he preaches is an exceptional man. I am sure I could instruct a score of people in what is right better than I could be one of the score to always do what is right myself. The head may attempt to make rules to govern the

6

passions, but a fiery temperament will not be bound by any cold-blooded rules. Hot-headed youth, like a hare about to be trapped, escapes rules and proverbs simply by leaping over them. But this kind of conversation is not the sort of thing that will be of any aid to me in the choice of a husband. Alas, that word "choice." I have no choice in the matter, either of refusal or acceptance. In such a manner can the wishes of a dead parent still rule the wishes of a living daughter. Do you not think it a cruel fate that it is out of my power either to accept or reject according to my own heart?

Nerissa: Your father was a good man all his life, and those who live good lives do not devise ill at their death. Therefore, there is good in this lottery. This plan of his, which seems but mere chance, no doubt had a deep meaning. He has most probably arranged so that none but a true lover would think of choosing the right casket out of the three. And, thus, the true lover will become your husband. But how is your heart inclined toward any of these noble suitors who have already arrived?

Portia: Let me hear all their names, and I will tell you what they are like as you do so. You will be able to judge accurately my love for them as I describe them.

Nerissa: To begin with, there is the Prince of Naples.

Portia: Ah! Now there is a fine young animal, and animals are all his conversation. He thinks it is a great addition to his other good qualities that he can shoe his own horse.

Nerissa: Next we have the King's officer, the Count of the Palace.

Portia: He is much too solemn. His pompous manner seems to imply that he is doing a great favor in becoming a suitor at all. He will not even laugh at a jest. If he is so grave as to be almost discourteous now that he is young, I am afraid that when he is old he will be like Heraclitus, always sunk in melancholy. An image of a skull and crossbones would make a more cheerful husband than that. Heaven preserve me from having to accept either him or the Prince!

Nerissa: Then what do you say to the Frenchman, Monsieur Le Bon?

Portia: Well, as Heaven saw fit to make him a man, I suppose we must call him one, as he is a piece of God's handiwork!

Nay, I did not mean to be irreverent, but he is worse than the other two. He thinks even more of his horses than the Prince of Naples. He frowns worse than the Count. He is 50 different men in his own person, and, yet, is not manly himself. He is so mercurial that if he hears a bird whistle he will dance to it. If he feels inclined to fight, he will take his own shadow for an adversary. Indeed, if I wedded him, I would have a score of husbands. I would not be the least angry if I found he did not want me, for I could never return his love, even if he doted upon me.

Nerissa: Then what have you to say to young Falconbridge, the English baron?

Portia: You know very well that I have nothing to say to him, for we do not understand the other's language. He does not know either Latin, French or Italian. As for my English, you would be able to declare an oath how little I know of that. He is a fine-looking fellow, but no one can be expected to live with a picture only! And how strangely he is dressed! He wears an Italian doublet and breeches of French fashion. He seems to have gone to Germany for his cap and to every land under the sun for his manners.

Nerissa: Then what is your opinion of his neighbor, the lord from Scotland?

Portia: My opinion is that he is a very kind-hearted and generous fellow; when the Englishman lent him a box on the ear, he swore he would pay him again as soon as he could. And, as in duty bound, I believe the French lord added his assurance that he would assist in seeing the debt paid.

Nerissa: Then how do you like the Duke of Saxony's nephew from Germany?

Portia: I dislike him intensely in the morning, though he is sober then, but more intensely still later in the day, when he has taken too much liquor. Even at his best, he is a very inferior specimen of a man. At his worst, there is little to distinguish between him and the brutes. Even should the worst happen to me that could happen, I trust I shall manage to do without him.

Nerissa: But, if he should come forward to make the choice and should happen to take the right casket, you would be disobeying your parent's wishes if you did not accept him.

8

Portia: Then, to save me from such a catastrophe, I beg you to place a tall goblet of wine on the wrong casket, for he would choose whichever casket held the wine, even if Satan himself were inside it. Whatever I do, I will never knowingly marry a drunkard.

Nerissa: Dear lady, you may set your fears at rest concerning these gentlemen, for they have told me that they mean to leave you and not press their courtship further, unless your father's decree concerning the caskets can be set aside, and they may court you in an ordinary way.

Portia: I will never consent to be won in marriage on any other conditions than those laid down by my father. Even if I were to live until I would be as ancient as the Sibyl, I would never wed except in that manner, but would die a virgin like Diana. It is a pleasure to hear that the suitors you have mentioned have so much sense, for I am overjoyed to hear of their leave-taking. May Heaven bless their journey.

Nerissa: Have you forgotten a young Venetian, who once came here with the Marquis of Montferrat? He was a soldier and an educated man. He came when your father was alive.

Portia: Oh, yes! I remember him. If I am not mistaken, his name was Bassanio.

Nerissa: You are right, my lady. I may not be very wise, but, in my opinion, he was more worthy to win a beauteous wife than any other man I have seen.

Portia: I have not forgotten him. Nor have I forgotten that he seemed all that you say.

[Enter a servant.]

Well? What have you to say?

Servant: The foreign gentlemen wish to see you, lady, to bid you farewell. An advance courier is here from another one. He informs us that his master, the Prince of Morocco, will arrive tonight.

Portia: I would be happy to hear that news if only I could welcome him as joyfully as I can say good-bye to the others. I cannot like a man with so dark a skin, even if he had the disposition of a saint. I would rather he hear my last dying confession than wed me.

Go on, fellow. Let us go, Nerissa. As fast as we say farewell to one suitor, another comes seeking admission.

[Exit.]

9

ACT I • SCENE 3

[Venice. A public place.]
[Enter Bassanio and Shylock.]

Shylock: Three thousand ducats. I understand.

Bassanio: Yes, sir, and I wish the loan for three months.

Shylock: You wish it for three months, yes.

Bassanio: And, as I have already said, Antonio will be security for it.

Shylock: Antonio security for it, yes.

Bassanio: Can you serve me in this? Will you oblige me? Will you let me know whether you can do it or not?

Shylock: You want 3,000 ducats for three months, and Antonio will be security for it.

Bassanio: Tell me at once whether you will do it or not.

Shylock: Antonio is a man of credit.

Bassanio: Have you ever heard anyone say otherwise?

Shylock: Oh, no! Not at all! I only meant you to understand that I know he is wealthy enough to repay me. At the same time, a great part of his wealth is exposed to the uncertainty of the seas. One of his ships is on its journey to Tripoli, and another eastward to the Indies. Also, from the conversation of the merchants on the exchange, I learn that others of his ships are voyaging to England, Mexico and various other distant places. But ships are only made of timber and are apt to be broken. Mariners are liable to be drowned, being merely human beings. Then there are thieves and robbers of all kinds, on land and on the waters. Also, all the dangers of the deep from rocks, gales and tempests. Still, Antonio's credit is good. I think I may accept him as security.

Bassanio: Certainly you may, without doubt.

Shylock: I shall make very certain and will leave myself no doubt on the matter. I will consider the matter. I would like to see Antonio himself.

Bassanio: That you may easily do if you will meet him at dinner.

Shylock: Indeed, and be obliged to see before me the flesh of the pig, which is, to us, unclean, and into which the Nazarene you believe in sent the evil spirits! No, I do not object to trade with you, to meet and converse wth you and so on. But I will never partake of food or drink with you or join with you in prayer. What tidings is there among the merchants? Ah! Who is this coming toward us?

[Enter Antonio.]

Bassanio: It is Signior Antonio himself.

Shylock: *[Aside.]* What a contemptible-looking fellow he is! I detest him, partly because he is a Christian but more because of his mean practice of lending money for nothing. And so we are obliged to ask a lower rate of interest for our money than we would otherwise be able to charge. If I can only get the opportunity to overthrow him, I will take ample satisfaction for my long-standing hatred of him. He looks upon our holy race with contempt. And, among the merchants, in the general meeting place, where there are many to hear, he criticizes and derides me. He pours contempt on me, my dealings and my hard-earned gains, which he says are close to extortion. May my tribe forfeit every blessing if I do not repay him for all this!

Bassanio: Well, why do you not answer, Shylock?

Shylock: I am thinking how much I have in hand at present. And, as nearly as I can remember, I fear I am unable to get the whole of the 3,000 ducats at once for you. But this is no matter. There is a rich merchant of our tribe, whose name is Tubal, from whom I can obtain the money I require. But wait a moment! What was the time for which you wished to borrow it? *[To Antonio.]* A fair greeting to you, worthy sir. We were just speaking of your honor.

Antonio: Although I make it a rule, Shylock, neither to charge interest on the lending nor pay it on the borrowing of money, for this once I will break my rule to be able to give my friend the money he is in immediate need of. Have you told him yet, Bassanio, the sum you require?

Shylock: Yes, yes, I know — three thousand ducats.

Antonio: And we require it for three months.

Shylock: I did not remember. But, of course, you said so before. Very well, you will give me your promise. But wait a moment. Did you not say that you never paid or charged interest upon money?

Antonio: I never do.

Shylock: When Jacob was keeping the flocks of his uncle, Laban — this Jacob was the third in descent from our pious father, Abraham, and, being cleverly helped by Rebekah, he became heir to all his father's possessions — yes, the third —

Antonio: Well, what about him? Did he do as you do, and charge interest?

Shylock: No, not exactly. He charged no interest in money. But notice, he made an agreement with Laban that all the lambs born with streaks and markings were to be considered as his wages. He made a good bargain of it and was successful. It is not wrong to be successful, if the prosperity is come by honestly.

Antonio: That was a pure speculation on Jacob's part. He had no control over it himself, but God guided and governed the event. But what has all this to do with the present matter? Is that story brought in to justify you in your extortionate ways or do you reckon your money to be like Jacob's flock?

Shylock: I do not know about that, but I can make it multiply as abundantly. Now hear me, sir.

Antonio: Notice this, Bassanio. Satan himself can use the words of Holy Writ to further his own ends. When we hear good and pious words spoken by one whose thoughts are wicked and sinful, we may compare that person to a man who has evil intentions in his heart, but who hides them under the mask of frank and pleasant manners, or to an apple whose outside is rosy and wholesome, but which is corrupt and decaying within. How strange a thing it is that the fairest outward appearance may often conceal the deepest untruthfulness!

Shylock: Three thousand ducats. It is no small amount of money. Now, what part of 12 is three? Then there is the percentage to consider —

Antonio: Well, Jew, can you oblige us in this matter?

Shylock: Again and again, Signior Antonio, among the merchants on the exchange, you have abused me and yelled at me, concerning my methods of business and the lending out of sums of money at interest. But I have always patiently tolerated your harsh words, merely shrugging my shoulders as I heard, for patient endurance is the strongest characteristic of our nation. You have spit upon my tunic in contempt and called me an unbeliever and cur. All this for no other reason than because I do as I choose with my own money and conduct my business according to my own ideas.

Now, it seems that you cannot do without me. Very well. You come with a request for money — you, who have spit upon me and spurned me out of your way as unceremoniously as you would kick a strange dog out at your door. And your request is for the loan of money! What shall be my answer? I ought to reply — "Has a dog money to lend? Are you likely to find 3,000 ducats in the possession of a dog?" Or again, I might say, bowing before you and speaking in the humble and submissive tones of a slave — "Noble signior, not many days ago you spit upon me. On another day, you pushed me aside with your foot. Again, you gave me the name of 'dog,' and, for all these instances of kindness and good manners on your part, I will let you have the money you require!"

Antonio: And I shall very probably do all this again. If you can let us have this money, you are not obliged to pretend friendship for us because of that. Indeed, no friend would ever take so much beyond what he lent to his friend. Let us have it openly and frankly as your foes. Then, should we fail to keep the agreement, it would pain you less to insist upon the full amount of the forfeit being paid.

Shylock: See now, how angrily you speak! I do not wish to be your foe. I desire your friendship, if you will give it. I want to be on better terms with you. I will no longer remember your insults and criticism of me but will freely let you have what you require for your immediate needs, and take not the smallest coin in interest for my loan. But you pay no attention to me. It is a really good offer.

Bassanio: If you mean that, it would indeed be good of you to offer it.

Shylock: I mean it, when I make this offer. Let us go together to a lawyer. There you shall give me a paper with your signature alone. And, for a jest, we will put in our agreement that if you are unable to let me have such certain sums of money back as we shall specify on the paper, by a certain date which we shall name, then let us name as the forfeit to be paid, an exact pound of the flesh of your body, which I am at liberty to take from any part I choose.

Antonio: I agree, certainly. I will give you my signature to that agreement and say that it is most kind of you to make the offer.

Bassanio: Never! I will not have you make such an agreement on my account. I would rather remain as poor as I am now and do without having my wants supplied at such a price.

Antonio: There is nothing to be afraid of, my friend. I shall never be called upon to pay the penalty. Long before the date of payment arrives, three months hence, my ships will have brought me many times the amount we are borrowing.

Shylock: O holy patriarch! Hear how these Nazarenes suspect evil! They are so unjust and oppressive to each other that they think everyone else is the same. I will only ask you to answer me this: what possible profit can it be to me to enforce the payment of such a penalty, if he is unable to repay me by the date named? It would not be worth so much to me, to have a pound of human flesh, as to have a pound of beef or of the flesh of sheep or goats. I repeat it, that I make this offer in order to show that I really desire Antonio's friendship. If he will accept it, well and good. If not, then farewell to you. But, for my sake, do not be unjust to me.

Antonio: Yes, I agree, Shylock, and will give you my signature.

Shylock: Then we will meet immediately at the lawyer's. Tell him of this jesting agreement and direct him to draw it up, while I go to get the money at once. I must also see that my house is safe, for I have left in charge of it a lazy fellow, and I fear he may not guard it well. Then I will come to you immediately.

Antonio: Hasten, good Shylock. *[Exit Shylock.]* Surely the Jew is becoming a Christian, he is showing so much goodness!

Bassanio: I do not trust fair words when we know the heart does not agree.

Antonio: Come, we will go to the lawyer. There is really nothing to fear. My vessels are due here some weeks before the date of payment.

[Exit.]

ACT II • SCENE 1

[Belmont. A room in Portia's house.]

[Flourish of trumpets. Enter the Prince of Morocco and his followers with Portia, Nerissa and others attending on them.]

Morocco: Dear lady, do not look upon me with dislike on account of my dark skin. It was bestowed upon me by the glowing sun, beneath whose direct and ardent rays I dwell. Let me be matched with any fair-skinned northerner, whose pale complexion shows him to belong to the land where the sun god's rays are so faint and feeble that they scarcely suffice to melt the frost and snow, and you would see, if our veins could be opened to prove our love to you, that in mine runs blood as red and courageous as that in his. The bravest of men, I swear to you, have felt fear before my expression, and the noblest and best of maidens in my own land have looked upon it with affection. I have no wish for a fairer complexion, except for one reason alone. I had rather remain this dark hue, unless the change would turn your thoughts with favor toward me, sweet lady.

Portia: As far as my own choice is concerned, I would not be influenced merely by what is pleasing to the critical eye of a maiden. But the choice does not lie with me. The fortune of my fate prevents me from exercising any freedom of choice. But, had circumstances been different, and had I not been limited and restricted by my father's wisdom and obliged to accept for a husband the one who shall succeed in winning me by the means he ordained, then, noble prince, you would stand as high in my regard as any of the suitors whom I have yet seen.

Morocco: I am grateful to you for so much. I beg you now to conduct me to the place where the caskets are, so that I may put my fate to the trial. I swear by my sword, which has done some famous deeds before now, for with it I slew a monarch of Persia who had already vanquished the renowned Solyman in three battles, that there is no danger I would not face if it might gain you, dear lady. Not even the fiercest look would make me fear, nor the most valiant warrior find me inferior to him in valor. For your sweet sake I would even dare the wrath of the female bear when her young ones are torn from her, or dauntlessly face the lion when, fierce with hunger, he goes forth in search of food. But alas, my fate depends not on my heart or sword but on blind chance. Set chance to be the judge and let Hercules' claim to superiority depend upon a throw of the dice, and even he might be vanquished by his squire if the squire throws a higher number! This may be my fate only, and, by mere mischance, I may lose the precious thing for which I strive, and lose my life for grief while someone more fortunate, though not more worthy, may obtain it.

Portia: You can find out by putting your fortune to the test. But you have the alternative of either leaving the matter alone altogether and not making the trial, or else, of having to vow that if, in making your choice, you do not obtain the right casket, you will henceforth give up love and never court another maiden. Consider carefully before you decide.

Morocco: I vow I will never court any lady but you. Let us go at once to make the trial.

Portia: You must first swear the oath in the holy shrine. Then, when we have dined, you shall put your fate to the test.

Morocco: May I be fortunate then, for when that is decided I shall be either the happiest or most miserable of men.

[Trumpets. All exit.]

ACT II • SCENE 2

[A street in Venice.]
[Enter Launcelot.]

Launcelot: In truth, my conscience will have to yield in this matter of whether I shall run away from the Jew whom I serve. The devil is close at hand, persuading me to do so. He whispers, "Gobbo" or "Launcelot Gobbo" or "worthy Launcelot" or "worthy Gobbo" or "worthy Launcelot Gobbo, make use of your heels and be off." My conscience replies, "Do not run. Be careful, good Launcelot. Be careful, good Gobbo," or, as I said before, "good Launcelot Gobbo, do not flee away. You should look upon the suggestion with contempt." Then the valiant devil persuades me to run off. "Away with you!" says he. "For heaven's sake, show some spirit and be off." But my conscience, hindering what my inclination would lead me to do, gives me this good advice, "My worthy friend Launcelot, as you are the child of a good father, or at least a good mother, for my father was not exactly free from some small taint, Launcelot, stay where you are, do not move.''

"Be off," says the devil again. "Do not stir," replies conscience. I say to my conscience that it gives me good advice. And I tell the fiend he gives good advice, too. If I obey my conscience, I remain in the service of the Jew who, preserve us, is a sort of evil one himself. If I leave his service, I would be obeying the real devil. But then, the Jew is the fiend in the flesh. And, if you ask my opinion, my conscience is very unfeeling to advise me to stay in the service of a fiend. The other advice is the kindlier, so I will obey it. I'll use my legs as the fiend advises me and be off.

[Enter Old Gobbo, with a basket.]

Gobbo: Tell me, I beg you, young sir, which way I must go to reach master Shylock's house.

Launcelot: *[Aside.]* By all that is wonderful, here is my own old father. Now, as he will not be able to recognize me, as he is more than half blind, being, indeed, scarcely able to see at all, I will try the experiment of having some fun with him.

Gobbo: I beg you, young sir, tell me which way I must go to reach master Shylock's house.

Launcelot: Take the next turning to the right, but the next to the left, and then at the next, do not turn at all but turn straight to the house.

Gobbo: That is a difficult direction to follow, by the saints. Do you know, sir, whether a certain Launcelot, who lives with the Jew, is still there?

Launcelot: Are you speaking of the young gentleman called Launcelot? *[Aside.]* Now observe. I shall fetch the tears to his eyes! Are you speaking of the young gentleman?

Gobbo: No young gentleman, sir. His father is only a poor man. Though I tell you myself, he is very honest but very poor. Yet, thank heaven, he has enough to live upon.

Launcelot: Well, whatever his father is, we will not concern ourselves with that. We are speaking of the young gentleman.

Gobbo: Yes, young sir, of your acquaintance, plain Launcelot.

Launcelot: That is, my good fellow, you are speaking of the young gentleman known as master Launcelot!

Gobbo: I am speaking of Launcelot, if it please your honor.

Launcelot: Therefore, of master Launcelot. Well, father, you need not speak of him any more. For, imitating the scholars who speak of such learned things and talk of the Fates, and Clotho and her sisters, I may tell you that young master Launcelot has departed this life and gone to paradise. To speak plainly, he is dead.

Gobbo: By St. Mary, may heaven forbid! He was my only support, the prop of my declining years.

Launcelot: Am I your idea of a prop — a support to hold a house up, a mere staff, a club? Do you not recognize your own son, father?

Gobbo: Alas! I know nothing about you, young sir. It is Launcelot whom I wish to hear of. Tell me, I beg you, whether he is really dead or not.

Launcelot: Have you not recognized me yet?

Gobbo: Unfortunately I cannot see you. I am nearly blind.

Launcelot: That is no drawback, for even if you could see, you might not recognize me. It is not every parent who can be sure of his own children. But indeed, father, I can tell you about your Launcelot, but you must bless me first. Facts are sure to reveal themselves. One cannot hope to conceal a murder, though one might be able to conceal a child. But everything is revealed in the end.

Gobbo: Do not kneel to me, young gentleman. I cannot believe that you are my son, Launcelot.

Launcelot: Argue no more about it, but bless me at once, for I am now, always have been and always shall be your son, Launcelot.

Gobbo: I cannot believe that to be true.

Launcelot: I do not know what I am to understand by that. But this I am sure of — that my name is Launcelot, that I serve Shylock the Jew and my mother is your wife, Margery.

Gobbo: My wife is certainly called Margery, so if you are really Launcelot her son, then you are my own son. Praise be to Heaven! How long your beard is! Dobbin the horse has not so much for a tail as you have for a beard.

Launcelot: Then Dobbin's tail appears to be growing upward. The last time I saw him, his tail would much more than equal my beard.

Gobbo: Heavens! How you have altered! How do you get on with the Jew? I have a gift for him here. Do you get on well with him?

18

Launcelot: Oh, fairly well. But I have made up my mind to leave him, so my mind will give me no peace until I have put a considerable distance between us. He is a thorough Jew. I would rather see someone bring a rope to hang him with than a gift for him. He half-starves me; you might feel all my ribs with your finger. It is very fortunate that you have arrived. Let me take the gift to a certain Signior Bassanio. His servants are well-treated and handsomely clothed. I will enter his service, or else I will be off and travel to the world's end. What a splendid chance! Here is Bassanio himself. Come, father, go and speak to him. I'll leave the service of Shylock this very moment.

[Enter Bassanio, with Leonardo and other followers.]

Bassanio: Very well, I agree. But see that it does not cause our meal to be any later than five o'clock. Send these letters to the persons to whom they are addressed. Give orders that the new outfit for my servants be begun immediately and tell Gratiano that I wish him to come to my rooms at once.

[Exit a servant.]

Launcelot: Go and speak to him, father.

Gobbo: Heaven send your honor every blessing!

Bassanio: Many thanks! Do you wish to speak to me?

Gobbo: Yes, sir. My son here, a poor fellow —

Launcelot: Not so very poor, sir. I have been a servant to the wealthy Shylock, and I would like, as my father will tell you—

Gobbo: His chief desire is to enter the service of —

Launcelot: Truly, the beginning and the end of the whole matter is, I am Shylock's man, and my great and chief wish is, as my father will tell you—

Gobbo: And my son and his employer, saving your presence, sir, scarcely get on well together —

Launcelot: Indeed, to put the matter shortly, the fact is that Shylock having done me an injury, as my father, who is, I trust, an honest man, will inform you —

Gobbo: I have brought some pigeons, which I would like to give your honor as a present, and I only request that —

Launcelot: In fact, the request is concerning me, sir, as this honest man will tell your honor. He is an honest man, though a poor man, and my father.

Bassanio: One at a time, please. What is it that you wish?

Launcelot: To enter your service, signior.

Gobbo: That is the heart of the whole matter, my lord.

Bassanio: I am acquainted with you, and your request is granted. Your master, the Jew, was speaking of you today and recommended you as worthy of a better job, if it is, indeed, any advantage to you to leave the employment of a rich master in order to serve a much poorer one.

Launcelot: You, signior, and the Jew each have a share of the old saying that tells us that "The grace of God is wealth enough," for he has the riches, and you have the favor of God.

Bassanio: Very well said! Take your old father with you and bid farewell to the Jew, then find your way to my house. Let him have a suit more elaborately trimmed than the other servants have. Be sure that this is attended to.

Launcelot: Come along, father. I must have you to speak for me, I can do no talking. I could never persuade anyone to take me, oh no! Really, I do not believe there is a single person in the land with a better fortune shown on his palm. I am ready to swear it. I see a very plain line of life, and also a few wives, about a score of widows and maidens. Oh, that is not much for one man. And here I see I shall be in peril of drowning, but I shall be saved. A wonderful thing indeed, to escape drowning only to fall a victim to marriage. Marvellous fortunes! However, I will acknowledge that Dame Fortune is kind this time, though she is a woman. Come along, father. It will not take me more than an instant to bid farewell to the service of Shylock!

[Exit Launcelot and Old Gobbo.]

Bassanio: Do not forget this, I beg, worthy Leonardo. When you have purchased these things and seen them carefully placed in readiness for us, come back as quickly as possible, for tonight I am entertaining all my greatest friends at my house. Hasten!

Leonardo: I shall do all to the best of my ability.

[Enter Gratiano.]

Gratiano: Is signior Bassaino here?

Leonardo: Yes, sir, he is walking yonder.

[Exit.]

Gratiano: Signior Bassanio!

Bassanio: Gratiano!

Gratiano: I have a request to make.

Bassanio: It is granted already.

Gratiano: Do not refuse me. I wish to go with you to Belmont.

Bassanio: Well, then, I suppose I must allow you. But listen, Gratiano, you are a little noisy and unrestrained in your behavior, and rather rough. Now, these qualities suit you very well, as they agree with your disposition, and we, your friends, do not dislike them in you. But in the eyes of strangers and to those unacquainted with you, they would appear too free and perhaps a little disorderly. I beg you, therefore, to take a little trouble to keep down your wild and exuberant spirits, and exercise a little moderation. Otherwise, I may be in danger of being misunderstood at Belmont. And, being judged by the companions who are with me, may lose all chance of success in my wooing.

Gratiano: Listen, Signior Bassanio! I promise to behave in a most staid and solemn manner. I will converse gravely and very seldom use an oath. I will carry religious books about with me and look most sedate. And, during grace before meals, I will veil my eyes with my hat in this manner and solemnly say "Amen." I will do everything that politeness demands, and follow all the customs of good manners, as though I were carefully trying to please my grandmother by showing a staid and serious behavior. If I do not faithfully keep my word in this matter, never believe me again.

Bassanio: Very well, we shall see how you behave.

Gratiano: Oh! But I do not count tonight in! You must leave out tonight. You must not judge me by my behavior tonight!

Bassanio: No, I shall not do that. I should be sorry to see you staid and solemn tonight. I would much prefer to see you in your wildest spirit and your most amusing humor, for those who are coming are looking forward to a night of mirth. Adieu for the present. I have some affairs I must attend to.

Gratiano: I also must go, for Lorenzo and some other friends are waiting for me. But we shall see you at our evening meal.

[Exit.]

ACT II • SCENE 3

[A room in Shylock's house.]
[Enter Jessica and Launcelot.]

Jessica: I wish you were remaining in my father's service. This

21

house is a place of misery, and your lively spirits made it a little less dull and monotonous. Good-bye, then, take this piece of money. When you go to Signior Bassanio's house, you will see Lorenzo among his guests. Deliver this note to him without letting anyone notice it. Good-bye. I do not wish my father to see me speaking to you.

Launcelot: Farewell, lady. My sorrow prohibits me from saying all that I would. My lovely heathen, my dearest Jewess, farewell. My tears of grief overcome me, more than a man should allow. Farewell!

Jessica: Adieu, good Launcelot.

[Exit Launcelot.]

Alas! How wicked of me to feel it a disgrace to be the daughter of my own parent! But, though I cannot help my relationship, I need not copy his behavior. If you keep your word, my Lorenzo, the struggle between love and duty will soon be over, and I shall be your beloved wife and leave my Jewish faith for Christianity.

[Exit.]

ACT II • SCENE 4

[A street.]
[Enter Gratiano, Lorenzo, Salerio and Solanio.]

Lorenzo: We can slip out unperceived while the others are engaged at supper, go to my rooms and there change our clothing. We can put on our disguise and be back here again in a very short time.

Gratiano: We have not had time to prepare for it properly.

Salerio: We have made no arrangements yet even for torches, or servants to carry them.

Solanio: This is a wretched affair, unless it is thoroughly well-managed and beautifully arranged. If that is not done, in my opinion, the frolic is better left alone.

Lorenzo: We have plenty of time to obtain the necessary equipment. It is still two hours before the time.

[Enter Launcelot, with a letter.]

Well, good Launcelot, what tidings have you?

Launcelot: If you will be good enough to break these seals, the letter will explain itself.

Lorenzo: That handwriting is familiar to me and so is the lovely hand that wrote it. The hand is fairer than the white paper and more beautiful than the writing.

Gratiano: It is tidings from a beloved one, then!

Launcelot: I will go now, sir.

Lorenzo: Where are you going?

Launcelot: Well, sir, I am going to carry an invitation from my new employer, the Christian Bassanio, asking my former master, Shylock the Jew, to supper.

Lorenzo: Wait a moment. Here, this is for you. Say to Jessica, unknown to anyone else, that I shall keep my word. She may rely on me.

[Exit Launcelot.]

Well, my friends, do you agree to arrange to join the revels tonight? I have a torchbearer for myself already.

Salerio: Yes, indeed, I will see about the arrangements at once.

Solanio: And I will do so, too.

Lorenzo: Come to Gratiano's house in about an hour, and we two will be there.

Salerio: That is a very good plan.

[Exit Salerio and Solanio.]

Gratiano: Your note was sent by the lovely Jewess, was it not?

Lorenzo: I see I must let you know all about it. Yes, she has told me what arrangements she has made for fleeing from Shylock's house, the amount of money and jewellery she can bring with her and the clothing in which she will disguise herself as a page-boy. She has also given me instructions as to my part in the escape. I am certain that if Shylock should ever get to paradise, it will only be by means of the sweet Jessica! And any harm or ill fortune that ever happens to her will only be because she happens to be the daughter of an unbelieving Jew! Come, let us go together. You can read the letter as we go. I told you I had a torchbearer. It shall be lovely Jessica, disguised as my page.

[Exit.]

ACT II • SCENE 5

[In front of Shylock's house.]
[Enter Shylock and Launcelot.]

Shylock: Well, you will soon find out by your own experience that Shylock and Bassanio are two very different persons —

Jessica! You will not be able to eat so much as you have done here, Jessica — or lie so long lazily slumbering, or wear out so many suits. Come, Jessica, do you not hear me?

Launcelot: I say, Jessica!

Shylock: How dare you call her! I gave you no orders to do so.

Launcelot: No, but your honor always used to say that I could never do anything unless I was told.

[Enter Jessica.]

Jessica: Did you call me, father? What do you wish?

Shylock: I am invited out to supper this evening, my daughter. I give my keys into your charge. But why should I accept this invitation? They did not invite me because they care for my company, but merely to deceive me into thinking that they esteem me highly, or to coax me into being indulgent to them. Well, then, I will go as their enemy and get all I can out of the extravagant Nazarenes. My daughter, take great care of the house. I have a strong disinclination to leave the house. I feel that some misfortune is threatening my peace of mind. Last night I dreamed about moneybags, a sure sign of evil.

Launcelot: Oh, sir, I beg you to come. Signior Bassanio is looking for your "reproach."

Shylock: And I am expecting his "reproaches" soon.

Launcelot: And I believe they have been making some arrangement. I will not tell you what it is, but if you should happen to be shown some sports, then that was what it meant when my nose bled last Easter Monday, early in the morning, happening to be on Ash Wednesday afternoon four years ago!

Shylock: Oh! Are there to be revels? Listen to me, Jessica. Fasten up the house securely and do not go up to the windows when you hear the hateful shrieking of the fife and the sound of the drum. Do not be seen by all the crowd, staring at painted idiots. Shut up the ears of the house. That is, close the windows, that no sound may enter. I will not have my quiet abode filled with the noise of such empty folly. I vow by the staff of our father, Jacob, I have a very great reluctance to go out to any feast tonight. However, I am resolved to go. You, fellow, return to your master and tell him I am coming.

Launcelot: I will be there before you, sir. Lady, notwithstanding what he says, be sure you look out the window, for a certain Nazarene will pass by who will be well worth your looking for.

[Exit.]

Shylock: What is that silly gentile talking about?

Jessica: He is only saying good-bye to me.

Shylock: He has a good heart, though he is such a fool, but he eats too much. He is far too slow and sleepy-headed. That is why I am sending him away, for I cannot have lazy people in my house. I am sending him, also, to a master whom I would like to see ruined, and whom I hope he will help to ruin, by helping to spend the money for which he is in debt to me. Now remain indoors, my daughter. I may change my mind, and come home quickly after all. Remember what I have told you and fasten the house up carefully. The old saying always holds good to a careful mind, "Leave all secure, and you will find all secure."

[Exit.]

Jessica: Good-bye. And, unless I have very great bad luck, you have lost your child, and I have no longer a parent.

[Exit.]

ACT II • SCENE 6

[Enter Gratiano and Salerio, wearing masks.]

Gratiano: It was under this shed that Lorenzo told us to wait for him.

Salerio: The time that he named will soon be past.

Gratiano: It is most wonderful that he should be behind time. Those who are in love generally rush to the meeting place long before the appointed hour.

Salerio: Yes, the doves that draw the chariot of the goddess of love speed far more quickly when they are journeying to bind new love more firmly than they do when love is once pledged and certain.

Gratiano: That is true in every case. No one is so eager on leaving a banquet as he was when he came to it. You will not find even a horse that will travel again over the same road on its return journey with the same energy and animation with which it set out. It is the case with everything in the world. The pursuit of any desired object is a more enjoyable

25

task and gives far greater pleasure than the enjoyment of it after it has been captured or attained. Look at the gaily decorated vessel sailing out from the harbor like a high-spirited youth setting forth to see the world, with the wild breezes playing among the sails. Then look at it on its return, like the spendthrift youth, with torn and ragged sails, frame battered and almost ruined by the same wanton gales!

Salerio: You can finish your speech later on. Lorenzo is approaching.

[Enter Lorenzo.]

Lorenzo: Forgive me, my dear friends, that I stayed so late. It was entirely on account of business matters that I was obliged to keep you waiting. If ever you wish to do what I am doing tonight and steal away a fair lady to be your wife, I will wait as long as you have done, to help you on that occasion. Come along. This is the house where my Jewish father-in-law lives. Hallo! Is there anyone within?

[Enter Jessica, above, in boy's clothes.]

Jessica: Who is that? I am sure I recognize the voice, but I would like to hear you say who you are, so that I may be absolutely sure.

Lorenzo: It is Lorenzo, your lover.

Jessica: Yes, you are Lorenzo, I see. Therefore, you are most surely my love, for you are the one I love above all. But who can tell whether you love me as much, Lorenzo?

Lorenzo: Your own heart tells you that, beloved. And God in heaven has heard our vows.

Jessica: Don't miss this little casc, when I throw it. You will find it worth the trouble of catching. I am not sorry that you cannot see me very clearly in the dusk, for I feel exceedingly shy in my new garments. However, it is proverbial that lovers' eyes are blinded so that they are not able to see the pleasing extravagances that love leads them into. Even the little love god himself would be shocked, I am afraid, if he saw me changed by these garments into the likeness of a youth.

Lorenzo: Come down into the street. You are to take the part of my torchbearer in the masquerade tonight.

Jessica: Must I, then, hold a light to show up my dreadful behavior? My deeds themselves are, truly, much too open to the light and should be hidden. To take the part of a torchbearer will reveal me to the sight of all, and I ought to be concealed.

Lorenzo: You are quite sufficiently concealed by your most charming disguise. Do not delay any longer. The time is flying, and the darkness will soon cease to shelter us. Also, they are waiting for us at the banquet that Bassanio is giving.

Jessica: I will come at once, as soon as I have locked up the house securely, and enriched myself with a little more money.

[Exit above.]

Gratiano: I vow by my hood, the maiden is too good to be a Jewess. She is a real gentile!

Lorenzo: Never trust me, if I do not adore her! If I have estimated her correctly, she is not lacking in wisdom and good sense. If my eyes tell me truly, she is beautiful, and she has shown to me that she is faithful and constant. So, thus, I shall keep her image in my faithful heart as constant, beautiful and wise.

[Enter Jessica, below.]

Ah! You are here. Come, friends, let us go. Our comrades, who are to share our sports, must now be waiting for us.

[Exit with Jessica and Salerio.]
[Enter Antonio.]

Antonio: Who is that?

Gratiano: Is it you, Signior Antonio?

Antonio: Gratiano, you ought to be ashamed! It is late, and you keep all the rest of the company waiting! But are you here alone? Where are your companions? There will be no revels tonight. The wind has changed and is now favorable to Bassanio, so he must depart immediately. There have been a score of us looking for you.

Gratiano: I am delighted to hear this. You could have given me no better news. Nothing will give me greater pleasure than to set out on our voyage at once.

[Exit.]

ACT II • SCENE 7

[Belmont. A room in Portia's house.]
[Flourish of trumpets. Enter Portia with the Prince of Morocco, and their followers.]

Portia: Let the curtains be pulled apart, and the different caskets be revealed to this illustrious prince. Now, Your Highness, choose which one you will.

Morocco: One, I see, is golden, and this is written upon it: "Whoever makes choice of me, shall be rewarded by obtaining what many people wish for." Another is of silver, and bears this assurance: "The one who makes choice of me will be rewarded according to his merits." The last is lead, and bears a caution quite as disagreeable as itself: "Whoever selects me must be prepared to give all and to risk everything." What will be the sign to tell me whether I have chosen rightly or wrongly?

Portia: If you select the right one, Your Highness, you will find my portrait within it. Should you happen to select that one, then with it you become possessed of me.

Morocco: Now, heavenly powers, guide my choice correctly! I will consider once more and retrace my readings of the words again. What is the inscription on this casket of lead? "Whoever selects me must be prepared to give all and to risk everything." "Give all," and get what in return? "Risk everything," and for what reward? For a piece of dull lead? Those who risk everything only run that risk if they have good reason to think they will reap a rich reward. But this inscription seems to bear a dismal warning. A man of a noble mind and high spirit will not lower himself to consider a worthless thing such as this appears to be. I shall risk nothing for so poor a reward.

Now let us see what the pure, white silver tells us. "The one who makes choice of me will be rewarded according to his merits." According to his merits! Stay for a moment at that word and consider. Let me judge myself impartially and consider what I am worth. If I take the esteem in which I am held as my standard of measurement, my merits may be very high indeed and even then, not be high enough to deserve this fair maid. But again, if I am too backward and too ready to depreciate myself, I lose my chance. "According to my merits." I am sure I merit the lady, alike in rank, in wealth and in manners. But, above all, I am worthy of her in my deep affection. Supposing I go no farther but make choice of this one!

I will look yet again at the inscription carved on the golden casket. "Whoever makes choice of me will be rewarded by obtaining what many people wish for." That again is Portia, everyone wishes for her. They come from every quarter of the globe to worship at the holy place that enshrines this living object of adoration. The far deserts of Persia and the immense wildernesses of Arabia are well-trod highways now, so thronged are they with noble gentlemen coming to see the lovely Portia. The ocean itself, which rears its proud crest and flings its spray to the very clouds, is no greater obstacle than a little stream to those adventurous strangers who come from other lands to see this lovely maid.

The portrait of this divine maiden lies in one of these caskets. Can it be supposed it is likely to lie in a dull, lead one? Cursed be the thought! Lead is not good enough even to form a coffin for her in the dark and gloomy tomb. Then must I imagine that she is hidden in silver, so much less precious than pure gold? Wicked, base thought! So precious a jewel could surely never be given any meaner setting than the finest gold. The English people have a piece of money called an angel, bearing the carved likeness of an angel. But in this casket the image of an angel rests on a couch of gold. Give me the key. I choose this casket, be the result what it will!

Portia: Here is the key, noble signior. If you find my portrait in that casket, you have won me for your wife.

[He unlocks the golden casket.]

Morocco: Oh, horror! What sight is this? A skull, and, in its eyeless socket, a roll of writing! Let me see what is written!

[Reads.] "Things that make the most brilliant show are not always the truest metal. Many times has that warning been sounded in your ears. For the sake of mere gold, hundreds have risked and forfeited their very existence. Costly tombs may be erected, and garnished with precious gold, but that gives them no real value. Decay and death are all that they contain. If your wisdom had equalled your courage, and had you united youthfulness of body to the

wisdom of riper years, your answer would have been a living woman, not a written scroll. As it is, you must depart. Your courtship is over."

It is over, truly, and all my pains are in vain. Adieu to the warm-heartedness of the lover. I must accept the cold comfort of the rejected. Farewell, dear lady, my sorrow is too great for many words. Those who have lost their heart's desire depart thus, sadly.

[Exit with his followers. Flourish of trumpets.]

Portia: A most welcome departure! Close the curtains once more, and let us go. I hope every suitor who is like him may be just as successful as he!

[Exit.]

ACT II • SCENE 8

[A street in Venice.]
[Enter Salerio and Solanio.]

Salerio: I have just seen Bassanio off on his voyage. The ship has gone, and Gratiano is in it, accompanying Bassanio, but certainly Lorenzo is not with them.

Solanio: The old rascal, Shylock, made such a disturbance that the Duke was obliged to attend to his demands and even accompanied him to look for Lorenzo on board the vessel Bassanio sailed in.

Salerio: He was not in time, however, to search it, for they had already put off from the land. But Antonio gave the Duke the most absolute assurance that Lorenzo had not sailed with them. While at the seashore, however, someone informed the Duke that the pair of lovers had been seen in a gondola.

Solanio: There never was such a disturbance, such an exhibition of passionate excitement and anger, in which all the causes of wrath were so mixed and confounded together, as in the outcry that the villain of a Jew made in the public street. "My child," he cried. "Oh, my money! Oh, my child! My child has gone! Has left me! And with a Christian! Oh, my Christian money! Let the law pursue them! My money and my child! Bags of money! Carefully preserved bags of gold, she has taken away. Precious gems, most valuable jewels, she has robbed me of! The law! The law! Let her be found and punished. She has them in her possession, my gems and my gold!"

Salerio: All the children in the town are at his heels, mocking his cries for his child, his gems and his money.

Solanio: Worthy Antonio had better pay his debt at the appointed time. Shylock will be little disposed to let him off, after this loss.

Salerio: That reminds me. A Frenchman with whom I was conversing yesterday told me that a richly laden ship from Italy came to grief in the narrow channel that divides his country from England. My mind instantly flew to Antonio's ships. Though I said nothing, I devoutly hoped it might not prove to be one of them.

Solanio: It would be a kindness on your part to let Antonio hear of this. But do not tell him such bad news without preparation, for it will cause him such distress.

Salerio: There is not a more generous-hearted man than Antonio in the whole world. I was there when he and Bassanio said farewell to each other. Bassanio said that he would hasten back as quickly as possible, but Antonio replied that he must make no such haste. "Do not perform your errand hastily or imperfectly on my account," he said, "or mar your wooing by hurrying back before it is properly accomplished. Wait for the most favorable opportunity to advance your suit and do not allow any thoughts of my agreement with Shylock to fill your mind, which ought to be entirely occupied with your lady. Allow yourself to be perfectly happy, and think only of showing your affection and devotion in the most suitable and appropriate manner." The tears rose to his eyes, and he said no more, but, with averted face, he took Bassanio's hand, his strong feelings of love expressing themselves in a lingering clasp. Then they separated.

Solanio: He seems only to care to live on Bassanio's account, he loves him so dearly. Come with me, I beg, and let us seek him and do our best to entertain him a little and cheer his sad spirit with some amusement.

Salerio: Yes, let us go.

[Exit.]

ACT II • SCENE 9

[Belmont. A room in Portia's house.]
[Enter Nerissa, with a servant.]

Nerissa: Make haste, I beg you. Open the curtains at once! The Prince of Arragon has already sworn to observe the conditions and is coming here immediately to make his choice.

[Flourish of trumpets. Enter the Prince of Arragon, Portia and their followers.]

Portia: There before you, Your Highness, you see the caskets. Should your choice fall upon the one that contains my picture, our marriage ceremony shall be performed immediately. But, should you choose wrongly, you must depart without further words.

Arragon: I have sworn to keep my word in three things. Firstly, I must never reveal to any other person which of the three caskets I selected. Secondly, if I do not win you, I must never court another lady. Thirdly, if I choose wrongly, I must depart at once without further words.

Portia: Every suitor who comes to take this risk in order to try to win my hand agrees to the same conditions.

Arragon: I come prepared for that. Good luck help me now and grant me my dearest wish! Here is gold, silver and worthless lead to choose from. What says this lead one? "The man who selects me must be prepared to give all and to risk everything." It must present a much better appearance than it does before I will risk anything for it! Let me look at the casket of gold. "He who chooses me shall obtain what many people long for." "Many people" — that probably means the crowd, the slow-witted rabble who have so little wisdom that they judge only by appearances and are led astray by outward glitter, never having been taught to follow any more trustworthy guide than their own foolish vision. The untaught eye never seeks the inner meaning of things but is content to remain on the outside, like the swallow, which, instead of seeking a sheltered place for its nest, constructs it in the most exposed places, unprotected from any accident that may occur. I will not follow the rabble, nor shall my choice be what "many men" long for. I do not choose to agree with the vulgar herd or be classed with the untaught crowd.

I therefore turn to the silver casket, which probably contains something precious within. Let me read again the words inscribed upon it. "He whose choice falls upon me shall be rewarded according to his merits." And rightly so! For none ought to be allowed to deceive and trick fate and their fellow men into paying them honor unless they deserve it. How happy a state would it be, if all rank, power and place were bestowed on the deserving, instead of being, for the most part, obtained by dishonorable and underhanded means, and if shining honor only adorned the brow of those whose deeds had fairly earned it! Many a man who now with uncovered head salutes his superior would himself be saluted with respect. And many a one who now issues orders to those who serve him would find himself among those who serve others. What baseness would be discovered among those families that are accounted the noblest. And how much goodness and virtue would be found amid those of fallen and decayed fortunes, which would be restored to their true place! However, I must return to my task of making a selection. "He whose choice falls on me will be rewarded according to his merits." Well, I will suppose that I have merit. Let me open this casket and see what my fate is to be.

[He opens the silver casket.]

Portia: You spend too much time over it, for all that you will obtain!

Arragon: What do I see! A picture of a half-blinded imbecile holding out a paper to me. What a difference between that creature and the picture I had hoped to see, of beauteous Portia! And what a difference between that wretch and the reward I longed for and thought that I merited! "He who makes choice of me shall be rewarded according to his merits." Do I indeed merit only that? Is a fool's head to be my only reward? Do I deserve nothing more?

Portia: You are the one who has committed the offence of making a wrong choice. You cannot, therefore, argue as to what your sentence ought to be. The offender who receives the sentence and the judge who pronounces it are never the same person. An offender cannot be the judge of his own case.

Arragon: Let me see what is written.

[*Reads.*] "The metal of which I am made was tried seven times in the flame, and seven times proved must that mind be that never commits an error of judgment. Some people find their happiness in shadows and follow after unrealities. Their happiness is therefore only shadowy and unreal. Many an unwise person's foolishness is hidden by his wealth, as this fool's head was concealed by the rich casket that enshrined it. Whatever companion you may have in life, your head is likely to be always that of a fool. You may take your leave now, your chance is over." To remain any longer would be to show myself more foolish than ever. All I have gained is another fool's head to add to my own.

Farewell, dear lady. I will abide by my promise and not rebel against my fate or weary you with further words.

[Exit Arragon and followers.]

Portia: So! There is another who has burnt himself in the flame. These people amuse me. They would be so wise, and they consider so carefully, and all the time they show themselves so utterly without wisdom. However, let us be thankful their foolishness has led them to fail in their choice!

Nerissa: The old proverb is right after all. It is fate that decides the matter, whether one is to be wedded or to be hanged.

Portia: Close the curtains once more.

[Enter a servant.]

Servant: Where is my mistress?

Portia: Your mistress is here. What do you wish to say, my master?

Servant: A young gentleman from Venice, lady, has just arrived. He comes as a forerunner of his master, to tell of his early arrival. And he brings most substantial greetings, namely, not only polite salutations and gracious speeches, but costly presents as well. I have never yet beheld so pleasing a messenger come on an errand of love. The sweetest spring day, with balmy breezes and gay with sunshine, coming to give us a foretaste of bright and bountiful summer, is not to be compared to this gorgeous messenger who rides in advance of his master.

Portia: I beg you, stop! You are so extravagant in your praises that I am dreading to hear you say presently that he is some

34

relative of your own, you seem so anxious that he should create a favorable impression. Let us go quickly, Nerissa. I am most impatient to behold this most attractive messenger of the little love god!

Nerissa: Oh, little god Cupid, grant that it may be Bassanio!

[Exit.]

ACT III • SCENE 1

[A street in Venice.]
[Enter Solanio and Salerio.]

Solanio: What tidings do they talk of on the exchange?

Salerio: The report that one of Antonio's vessels, with a valuable cargo, has come to grief in the waters that wash the English shores has not been disproved. It is on a most perilous sandbank called the Goodwin Sands, I believe. It has proved to be the grave of many a gallant vessel, if rumor speaks the truth.

Solanio: I only wish rumor may prove to be as big a liar in this story as any old woman who ever gossiped with her neighbors over her gingerbread cakes and told extravagant stories to astonish her hearers. But I fear it is only too correct, without wasting more words over the matter or beating about the bush, that excellent Antonio, noble Antonio — I wish I could find a description worthy enough to apply to him.

Salerio: Well, well, get to the end of your story.

Solanio: What do you say? To conclude, then, one of his vessels is lost.

Salerio: I devoutly hope that he will lose no more.

Solanio: Let me agree quickly and add my prayer to yours, before Satan has time to interfere and prevent it, for I see him approaching in the likeness of a Jew.

[Enter Shylock.]

Well, Shylock, what news is being talked of in the city?

Shylock: You know very well. Indeed, you know better than anyone that my daughter has fled.

Salerio: You are quite right. In fact, I am well-acquainted with those who provided the means for her flight.

Solanio: And you yourself, Shylock, were quite aware that she was grown up. It is the natural disposition of young birds to leave the nest when they are old enough.

Shylock: Who would have thought my own child would turn against me?

Salerio: She is as complete a contrast to you as black is to white, or as rich red wine is to pale Rhenish wine! But have you heard anything of Antonio's affairs, whether they are prosperous or not?

Shylock: That is another bad business for me. He has not enough money to pay his just debts. He is ashamed to show his face among the merchants. He is ruined — the man who came strutting among the traders in the marketplace so fine and proud! But let him beware! He used to scream at me for lending money out at interest. Let him see to it that he has enough to pay me. Let him see that he keeps his agreement. He used to lend money for the pleasure of doing a kindness. Let him see that he keeps his agreement.

Salerio: But, surely, if he is unable to pay, you would never insist on having his flesh! Of what possible use would that be?

Shylock: It would catch fish! Even if it were of no other use, it would satisfy my thirst for vengeance. He has not only brought me to shame, he has caused me to lose an immense sum of money. He has rejoiced when misfortune struck me, and mocked my successes. He despises my race, interferes with my dealings, turns my friends against me and incites my foes to do me further injury. And the sole motive for all this persecution is that I am a Jew! Is a Jew so different from everyone else? Are not a Jew's limbs and body, a Jew's feelings and emotions, a Jew's mind and heart as worthy of consideration as other people's? The same meat nourishes him, the same weapons wound him, the same sickness strikes him and the same remedies cure him. The same sunshine warms him, and the bitter cold of winter freezes him, just as it does any Christian.

Does not our blood flow if our skin be pierced? Do we not laugh if we are tickled? If we be poisoned, will it not kill us? And if an injury is done to us, shall we not long for vengeance? We are not different from Christians in other ways, and we will follow your example in that also. When a Christian is injured by a Jew, what course of action does the Christian take? Does he follow the teaching of his own creed and suffer it, rather than do harm to another? No! He avenges himself upon his enemy. Then, if the case is reversed, what should a Jew do, if he follows the Christian example? Avenge himself upon his adversary! And I will do so. I will take the course of action that you Christians have taught me, and it will be strange if I do not improve upon the lesson!

[Enter a servant.]

37

Servant: Signiors, my master, Antonio, wishes to see you both at his house.

Salerio: We have been looking for him high and low.

[Enter Tubal.]

Solanio: Here is a second Jew. It would be difficult to produce a third to mate with them, unless it was Satan himself.

[Exit Salerio, Solanio and servant.]

Shylock: Well, Tubal, what tidings do you bring? Did you find Jessica in Genoa?

Tubal: No, I never saw her, though I had news of her frequently.

Shylock: Alas! Alas! She took a priceless diamond with her. I paid an immense sum for it in Germany. The evil fate of our nation has descended upon us at last! It never fell upon me before! There are hundreds of ducats lost in that one stone, and she has many others — valuable gems. I wish she were lying dead before me, adorned with her precious jewels! I wish she were being carried to her burial, and the money with her! And she cannot be found? Well! Well! After costing me so much to have her searched for! It is throwing good money away after bad, and I get nothing for my pains. I neither find my money and my jewels nor have the satisfaction of punishing my daughter. Every misfortune that happens seems to fall upon me. I am the only one who has to grieve. My tears are the only ones that fall.

Tubal: Nay, you are not the only one upon whom misfortune falls. When I was in Genoa, I was told that Antonio —

Shylock: Yes, yes, yes? What of him? Any bad news? Any bad news?

Tubal: That a vessel of his was wrecked on the way back from northern Africa.

Shylock: Thank Heaven! Do you think we may believe it? Do you think so?

Tubal: Yes. I talked with some of the rescued crew.

Shylock: How grateful I am to you for your welcome news! Where did you see them? Here in Italy?

Tubal: I heard in Genoa that Jessica had spent 80 ducats in one evening.

Shylock: Oh! You stab me to the heart! Eighty gold pieces at once! Eighty gold pieces! Gone forever!

Tubal: Several merchants to whom Antonio owes money trav-

38

elled with me on my return. It is their opinion that he will be obliged to go bankrupt.

Shylock: I heartily rejoice to hear it, and I will do him all the harm I can. I will torment him. I am delighted!

Tubal: Your daughter had bought a monkey from one of these men. He showed me a ring she had given him in payment.

Shylock: Shame on her! It is agony to me to hear this. That ring, with a turquoise in it, was one that her mother gave to me before we were married. I would never have parted with it for a whole forest full of monkeys!

Tubal: But it is certainly true that Antonio is ruined.

Shylock: Yes, indeed. I must not forget that. Go for me, Tubal, and engage a sergeant. Engage him for the week after next. If Antonio breaks his agreement, I will demand the payment on the forfeit. I will have his very heart. Hasten, kind Tubal, and do this for me. Then come to me at our place of worship. Hasten, worthy Tubal.

[Exit.]

ACT III • SCENE 2

[Belmont. A room in Portia's house.]
[Enter Bassanio, Portia, Gratiano, Nerissa and attendants.]

Portia: Stay awhile, I beg you, and let some days pass before risking a final decision. For, should you make a mistake in your selection, you must then leave me at once. I am conscious of feeling a strong desire that you should remain awhile, though I do not know whether that feeling is dictated by affection or not. You must judge for yourself whether dislike would be likely to prompt such a desire. But I would like to keep you near me for some weeks before you hazard a choice of the caskets. In that time, you might learn to know me better — and yet it is not proper for a maiden to disclose all her thoughts and feelings. It would be easy for me to let you know which casket to take, but I would be committing perjury, for I am under a solemn oath not to aid anyone's choice, and I will never commit so great a sin. But, for lack of my aid, you may choose wrongly and lose me. That would make me wish I had committed perjury.

Fie on the power of your eyes! They must have bewitched me, for I seem to be no longer myself. Half of me belongs to you, and the other half belongs to you — I mean to me. And, even then, if it did belong to me, it would still be yours. Alas, in these wicked days, it seems that people are not allowed to possess what rightly belongs to them! Thus I, who really belong to you already, may never be given to you. If that proves to be so, then it is not I who should be the sufferer, but fate, whose fault it is. I am talking too much, I know. But I only do it to prolong the time and put off the moment when you make your choice.

Bassanio: Let me make it now, for my present state of suspense racks me with torment.

Portia: The rack is for traitors. What treason is there in your affection? Let me hear it.

Bassanio: Fear is the only traitor to my love, I fear so greatly that I may miss the enjoyment of it. As for treason in reality, there is no more possibility of friendship between treason and my love for you than there is of snow and fire living in friendship together.

Portia: That is all very well, but I am afraid that declaration was made under pressure and may be no more to be trusted than the protestations of those who, being tortured on the rack, will declare anything to save their lives.

Bassanio: If you will assure me that you will give me life, I will declare the truth to you.

Portia: I agree, then. Declare it and live.

Bassanio: If you had said "Declare it and love," you would have summed up all the declaration I was about to make, for it was only to declare that I loved you. What delightful persecution I have to undergo, when my persecutor tells me what replies will best achieve my deliverance! But do not let us delay any longer. Take me to the caskets and let me put my fate to the test.

Portia: Hasten, then! One of the caskets encloses my picture. Your love, if it be true, will lead you to the right one. Nerissa, stand apart with the others. Bid the musicians play while Bassanio makes his selection. Should he fail to choose rightly, music will accompany his end, as the swan that is about to die sings sweetly in departing. And, in order that the likeness to a swan may be complete in every detail, the tears that I shall weep if he departs will represent the river that bears the swan away. But Bassanio may not fail. In that case, the music will be the joyful proclamation of a new king about to begin his reign. It will sound as sweetly as the melodious tones that gradually steal into the bridegroom's consciousness on the morning of his wedding day and bid him hasten to the happy ceremony.

See! He advances to the caskets as noble in bearing as Hercules himself but much more loving in heart than was that hero when he bravely rescued the maiden who was about to be offered in sacrifice to the dragon for the sake of the weeping Trojans. I represent Hesione, the maiden whose happiness depended on the hero. Nerissa and my maidens standing around are the women of Troy, looking with tear-stained faces to see the result of the gallant deed. Go forth, my hero! If thou art the victor, then my life is saved. The warrior who fights for his love has far less fear than I, who merely look on!

[Music while Bassanio comments on the caskets to himself.]

[Song.] Who can say where love has its origin! Does it spring from the feelings of the heart or from the approval of the intellect? What brings it first into existence, and on what is it fed and fostered? Answer and say! It springs to life in a glance of the eye, when the gaze alights on some pleasing form. It is nourished by the continued sight of the loved one, and then, alas, it often fades away as swiftly as it grew. Toll for the death of such swiftly passing love. I sound the first knell — ding, dong, bell.

All: Ding, dong, bell.

Bassanio: Thus may the realities of things be very different from the appearance they present to the world. Decorations and adornments of various kinds always have power to lead the multitude astray. The possession of a pleasing voice and attractive presence in a lawyer will, in a lawsuit, entirely hide any appearance of wrong or falsity in the cause he pleads, be it ever so rotten or unsound. The greatest heresies in religious opinion can be glossed over and their dangerous tendency concealed if some reverend-looking person with a sober expression gives them his approval and gravely quotes Scripture in support of them, hiding with outward embellishments the evil heart of the matter. Every wrong is wise enough to try to present at least the appearance of right. Many a cowardly fellow is as valiant to all outward appearance as the heroes of ancient days. But, could we see below the surface, we would find them nervous and faint-hearted, and as unreliable as the shifting sand, which gives way beneath the footstep it should support. The manly appearance is only cultivated in order to deceive the world into thinking them formidable.

When we examine beauty, we find that an imitation of it is easily obtainable and may be bought so much at a time. And, curiously, those who weigh themselves down with this false beauty are generally the lightest persons. Their shining hairdos, whose ringlets are tossed about by the playful breezes and make such a pretence of reality, have frequently been the possession of another who has long since lain in the tomb.

Thus, we see that outward adornments are always deceptive and lead into perilous waters. They are like the lovely veil that screens the dark face of the Indian. They are but the imitations of realities, the pretentious appearances used by the crafty to deceive even the most discerning. I will not, then, choose the showy casket of gold, the metal that King Midas coveted. Nor will I have the sickly, pale silver, the slave to every man's need, of which the common coins are made. I choose, instead, this insignificant lead, whose forbidding looks seem to imply that little may be looked for from its poor and worthless appearance. It makes no pretensions and may therefore possess the more real worth. Its unpretentious looks impress me more than the most fervent protestations. So this is my choice, and may it be a fortunate one and lead me to happiness!

Portia: *[Aside.]* Now love drives every other emotion far away! Mistrust has vanished. Despair, too soon anticipated, is gone forever. Doubt of the outcome and pale envy will trouble me no more! Oh, love, calm this wild delight, overwhelm me not with this rapture. Bestow your blessings with a less bountiful hand, or I will be altogether overpowered. I am afraid of such perfect bliss. It may prove too much for me!

Bassanio: What is this I see? *[Opening the lead casket.]* The likeness of the lovely Portia! Surely some divine being has created this image, which comes so near the reality! Is it only imagination that these eyes appear in motion? Do they appear to live and move only because my own do so? And see, too, these parted lips that the sweet breath divides. No harsher thing should come between so lovely a pair.

Her sunny tresses are so cunningly portrayed that men's hearts will be taken captive by their beauty and be held firmer than the tiny insects in a spider's web. It would be no marvel if the painter had found himself unable to present her lovely eyes at all, being so dazzled by their brightness. When he had painted one, it might well have power to steal the sight from his own eyes and render him unable to paint its fellow. But these poor words of praise are as far below the deserving of this lovely picture as the picture itself is inferior to the beauteous lady it represents. In this paper, here, my fate is contained and summed up for me to learn.

[Reads.] "May all those who do not judge by outward appearances be as fortunate as you have been, and make their choice as wisely! Now seek no farther for your happiness, let this suffice that has happened to you. If you are satisfied with it and feel that fate has brought you happiness, then go to your lady and confirm your choice with a kiss of love."

A courteous and generous writing! Sweet Portia, allow me! I do but obey the instructions of the scroll. I bestow a gift and receive one in return. I feel like one who is striving to win some contest. He hears the applause and the clamor of the crowd but is too bewildered by the struggle to be able to tell whether the applause is for him or not. Just so do I, loveliest Portia, stand, uncertain whether victory be mine until I receive confirmation of it from your own fair lips.

Portia: Here I am, Signior Bassanio, just as you see me. I do not pretend to be otherwise than as I appear to you. As far as my own wishes are concerned, I am content to be as I am. But, for your sake, I would like to be many, many times better, wealthier and more beautiful. I wish I were infinitely fairer and that my friends, my goodness, my possessions and my estates were beyond all telling, if that would raise me higher in your esteem. But all I can offer you in my own person is a mere nothing. I can give you only an untaught, unskilled maiden, who, however, is glad that she is still young enough to have time to improve. Better still, who has wit enough to be able to improve. And, best of all, who is fortunate enough to have such a teacher as you, Signior Bassanio, to whose care she will willingly yield her mind and heart, and from whom she will gladly learn.

All I possess, together with myself, now changes hands and is given to you, dear lord. A moment ago, I ruled over this house, governed my attendants and was mistress of myself and my own actions. Now, at this moment, I bestow them all upon you, my lord — mansion, servants and myself I give into your hands, as I give you this ring. If ever you allow it to pass out of your possession, if you should lose it or bestow it upon another, it will foretell the decay of our affection and give me the right to reproach you.

Bassanio: Sweet lady, your love and goodness render me speechless. I have no suitable words with which to thank you. I am overwhelmed by my emotions and feel bewildered. As the confused murmur of applause, which rises from the crowd on the conclusion of a well-delivered speech from some favorite ruler, is expressive of pleasure and yet incoherent and almost inarticulate, so my faculties seem to be unable to give expression to my great joy in any coherent speech. I can only say that, if you should ever hear that this gift of yours has left my finger, then you may know that my spirit has fled. Fear not, then, to say that Bassanio no longer lives.

Nerissa: My dear mistress and Signior Bassanio, we who have looked on at this fulfilment of our desires for your happiness, now wish to offer you our congratulations. May every happiness be yours!

Gratiano: Sweet lady and my dear lord, I hope that all the good you would yourself desire may be showered upon you. And I know that you will wish me the same. And please grant me this favor — that, when the ceremony is performed between you, my lord, and your dear lady, to bind you together in love, I may also celebrate my marriage at the same time.

Bassanio: I consent most heartily, provided you also obtain a wife.

Gratiano: Many thanks, my dear master. You have already been the means of my having obtained one. I am no less skilled than you in perceiving beauty. While you wooed Portia, I wooed her gentlewoman. We both made a speedy courtship, for I am no more inclined to delay than you are, sir. Your success or failure depended upon your choice of the right casket. So, as it happened, did mine. For, after I had exhausted myself in pleading and persuasion, and vowed affection until I could speak no longer, I obtained this concession at length, from this fair maid, that if it should be your happy fate to obtain Lady Portia, I would be made happy by the gift of Nerissa's love.

Portia: Does he speak truly, Nerissa?

Nerissa: Yes, madam, if it does not displease you.

Bassanio: And are you serious about this matter, Gratiano?

Gratiano: Yes, signior, truly in earnest.

Bassanio: We shall feel greatly complimented that your wedding is to take place at the same time as our festivities.

Gratiano: Who are these approaching? Here come Lorenzo and his little unbeliever! And our old acquaintance, Salerio, from Venice, is with them.

[Enter Lorenzo, Jessica and Salerio, a messenger from Venice.]

Bassanio: I bid you both heartily welcome to this house, if I may venture to do so yet, having only had the right to do so for such a very short time. Dear Portia, if you will allow me, I welcome these true friends and fellow citizens of mine with all my heart.

Portia: I add my greetings to yours, Bassanio, and welcome them cordially.

Lorenzo: You have our thanks, madam. Signior Bassanio, I had not intended to come to Belmont. But, I met Salerio, who was on his way here, and he begged me so earnestly to accompany him that it was impossible to refuse.

Salerio: That is true, signior, and I knew I had good cause to bring him here with me. Signior Antonio sends you greetings.

[Gives Bassanio a letter.]

Bassanio: Before I read this, tell me how Antonio is.

Salerio: I cannot say that he is ill, unless it be mentally. Nor can I pronounce him well, unless it be mentally. The letter he has sent will inform you of how he stands.

Gratiano: Go to that new visitor, Nerissa, and greet her with words of kindness. Salerio, I salute you. What tidings have you from our native town? How is Signior Antonio, our merchant prince? He will rejoice to hear that our enterprise, like Jason's, has been crowned with success. Like modern Argonauts, we have obtained our golden fleece.

Salerio: I wish that the success you have obtained could be able to supply the place of what Antonio has lost.

Portia: There must be bitter tidings in that letter, to make Bassanio look so pale. He must have lost someone greatly beloved by him, for, surely, nothing else could so greatly agitate a man with any self-control. See, his sorrow deepens. Tell me, Bassanio, I beg you. We two are now one, and so I ought to share in anything that happens to you. Tell me what the letter has brought!

Bassanio: Dearest lady, this letter contains some of the most unwelcome tidings that ever darkened the paper they were written on. Kind Portia, when I first disclosed my affection for you, I did not hide from you that I did not possess any great riches. I frankly confessed that my good birth was all I had to recommend me, and I spoke nothing but the truth. But, even when I claimed nothing more than that and told you that I owned no possessions, I was overstating my position. I ought to have said that I owned less than nothing, being in debt.

I am deeply indebted to a kind friend of mine. And this friend, for my sake, has given a bond to his worst foe, a man who hates him, solely in order that he might supply me with the money I needed. This letter seems to me Antonio's body, and the cruel words are so many stabs, each seeming to pour forth the lifeblood of my friend. But can it really be so, Salerio? Is not one of his enterprises successful? Have all his ships, in the many lands they sailed to, north and south, east and west, been wrecked on the ruining rocks? Have the perilous seas not spared one vessel?

Salerio: All have perished, signior. And, further, I learn that even if Antonio had a sufficient sum of money at once to pay off his debt to Shylock, he would not accept payment. I never saw any human creature so eager to bring about another's ruin. He gives the Duke no peace, but urges him continually to condemn Antonio. He accuses the governors of laziness in administering the laws unless they bring Antonio to trial. All Antonio's friends, all the most important men in Venice, and even the Duke himself, have used all their powers of persuasion, but without effect. He holds stubbornly to his malicious purpose of exacting the full penalty for the forfeiture of the bond.

Jessica: When I was at home, he has frequently declared, in my hearing, to other Jews who visited him that to have the penalty carried out and to be given the pound of flesh would give him more pleasure than to be paid the debt many times over. I am certain that Antonio is in grave danger unless the authority of the state is able to intervene and save him.

Portia: Is it the kind friend who supplied your wants, that is now in such peril?

Bassanio: My closest friend, the one whom I love above all others. Of a disposition that never tires of performing kind actions, of the sweetest and most generous nature and of a spirit more closely resembling the honorable Romans of old than anyone now living in the land.

Portia: What is the amount of his debt to Shylock?

Bassanio: He owes 3,000 ducats on my behalf.

Portia: Is that all? Pay him double the amount and let the bond be destroyed. Give him twice as much and then three times as much again, rather than let such a friend as you have described suffer the slightest injury because of my dear husband! Let us be wedded at once, that you may have a right to the money and then fly to your friend's assistance. You shall never have cause to mourn over the price you had to pay when you became my husband. I will give you money to free your friend from that insignificant debt a score of times over. Then, when that faithful friend is set at liberty, bring him here with you. Meanwhile, Nerissa and I will remain here and mourn your absence. Let us go at once, and then you must depart quickly, even the same day that we are wed. Be sad no longer but welcome your guests with a cheerful expression. I shall love you very dearly and value you most highly, since such a price has been paid so that I might wed you. But before we go, read to me what your friend has said.

Bassanio: *[Reads.]* "Dearest friend, my vessels have all perished, and I have but little else left. Those to whom I owe money are harshly pressing for its payment, and I am unable to keep my day of payment to Shylock. I have incurred the penalty that we agreed on when I signed the bond, and, since the payment of it means my death, I only wish to see you once again before I die. That will relieve you of any debt that you may owe to me. However, do as you will. If the affection you bear for me does not bring you to my side, do not let my request compel you to come."

Portia: O dear Bassanio, do all that is to be done quickly and hasten to his aid!

Bassanio: I will indeed hasten, since you are willing that I should go. But I will not sleep or take any rest until I return to you.

[Exit.]

ACT III • SCENE 3

[A street in Venice.]
[Enter Shylock, Solanio, Antonio and jailer.]

Shylock: Keep him well, jailer. Do not plead to me for mercy. This man was foolish enough to lend money for nothing. Guard him carefully, jailer.

Antonio: But listen once more, worthy Jew.

Shylock: It is useless to argue with me about the agreement. I insist on having it paid in full, and I have vowed that it shall be done. You gave me the name of "dog" before I had done you any injury. Now you see that the dog's teeth can bite! I will have the case judged by the Duke, who cannot allow the breaking of a signed agreement. It surprises me greatly that your jailer is so foolish as to bring you out because you asked him.

Antonio: I beg you, listen to what I have to say.

Shylock: I will not listen. All I want is my bond. It is useless attempting to change my mind. I insist on the agreement. I am not so stupid as to yield to persuasion or be shaken in my determination by the pleadings of anyone, much less give up my point at the request of Christians. Do not attempt to come after me. I will not talk with you. I insist on my agreement.

[Exit.]

Solanio: This is surely the most hard-hearted wretch that ever lived among human creatures.

Antonio: Say no more. I will make no more useless appeals to him. He has determined on my death, and I know full well the cause of his hatred. I have frequently been able to help those unfortunate creatures who were in his power through debt. When they came to me in their distress, I have delivered them out of his clutches. Hence, his dislike of me.

Solanio: Surely the Duke cannot permit this bond to hold good!

Antonio: The Duke will be obliged to let the law take its course. If he should interfere, from motives of pity or friendship or from any motive whatever, it would endanger the reputation of our state. And that, in view of the great number of strangers and foreign merchants who trade with us, would be most disastrous to our city. We cannot afford to have any accusations of injustice brought against us, because of our extensive trade and our relations with so many different lands. Leave me now. There is no hope for me, and I am so worn down, with all my anxieties and troubles that there will scarcely be a sufficient quantity of flesh left upon me by tomorrow to pay the forfeit to the murderous creature to whom I am in debt. Proceed, jailer, we may as well return. Heaven grant that my dear friend may arrive in time, and then I shall not grudge the price I pay.

[Exit.]

ACT III • SCENE 4

[Belmont. A room in Portia's house.]
[Enter Portia, Nerissa, Lorenzo, Jessica and Balthasar.]

Lorenzo: Dear lady, your conception of the pure and noble friendship that exists between Signior Bassanio and Antonio is a high-minded and worthy one. And, though I say it to yourself lady, you show how capable you are of sympathizing with exalted ideals in the noble way in which you have taken the sudden separation from your newly wedded husband for friendship's sake. But you would be still more ready to do this good deed if you were acquainted with the noble character of the man you are befriending, and knew the deep love he bears Signior Bassanio. You would then have greater joy in performing this generous act than you can reap from ordinary deeds of benevolence.

Portia: I have never had cause to regret any kind action I may have done, and I am certain I shall not need to regret this one. When two people are close friends, the love they have for each other being mutual, and finding their chief delight in each other's company, the two natures must have many things in common, and there must be a certain similarity of mind, behavior and disposition. From this, I argue that, as Signior Antonio is my husband's dearest friend, he must be as noble and worthy a gentleman as my husband. In that case, it is a very small sacrifice on my part to do all that is in my power to rescue a friend so like the one I love from a position of such distress. But this sounds too much like taking credit to myself for rescuing him. I will say no more but speak to you of other matters.

I give into your hands, Lorenzo, the entire management and care of this mansion during my husband's absence. I shall be absent also, for I have taken an oath that I will go to the neighboring convent, and there pass my days in religious exercises and holy meditation, with none but Nerissa as my companion, until our husbands reach home again. Please do not refuse this task, which my love obliges me to ask you to perform.

Lorenzo: I accept the task most willingly, and will perform all that you graciously desire.

Portia: I have already informed my servants of my intentions. They will look upon you and Jessica as their master and mistress until we shall return. Adieu, therefore, for a while.

Lorenzo: May your days be joyful and your meditations sweet!

Jessica: May every good be yours!

Portia: I return your good wishes with pleasure and good will. Adieu!

[Exit Jessica and Lorenzo.]

Balthasar, I have already proved you to be loyal and faithful. Show yourself in this instance to be still the same. Hasten with all the speed you are capable of to Padua. Bear this letter from me to my relative, the lawyer, Bellario. Then, be careful to bring whatever he gives you, papers and robes, as swiftly as possible, even with the speed of thought, to the public ferry that travels back and forth to Venice. Do not stay to talk about it. Go, and speedily. I shall arrive first at the ferry.

Balthasar: I shall do your errand as swiftly as possible, lady.

[Exit.]

Portia: Now, Nerissa, hasten with me! I have a plan to carry

50

out. I have not told you of it yet. We shall be where Signior Bassanio and Gratiano are, long before they dream of our being near them.

Nerissa: Will they know we are there?

Portia: We shall be in full view of them, but so clothed that they will be completely deceived and will think that we possess many qualities that we do not. When we two are dressed in youth's clothes, I am willing to bet that I shall look like the handsomer youth. I shall wear my dagger with a more gallant attitude and speak with the tones of a youth just arriving at manhood. My steps, instead of being short and quick, shall stretch out to twice their length, to imitate the stride of a man. I shall talk of brawls and fights in a careless, boastful fashion and tell stories of the many great women who have loved me and died of a broken heart because I did not love them in return; I could not help it; it was not my fault.

Then, I shall seem to be sorry for their fate and say that I grieve that they died for my sake! And so I shall go on, with many other little inventions, until people will believe that it is no more than a year ago since I left school. Oh, I know hundreds of the little ways of these very young and inexperienced youths, and I will try them all. But let us go at once to the carriage, which is already waiting at the entrance to the park. I will let you hear all my plans while we are on the way. We must not delay, for we must be many miles away before night.

[Exit.]

ACT III • SCENE 5

[A garden.]
[Enter Launcelot and Jessica.]

Launcelot: Yes, indeed. I assure you that I fear for you, because, you see, the wicked deeds of the parents have evil consequences for the children. I always spoke freely to you, and now I am telling you my thoughts on the subject. I really believe you will be lost! There is only one chance for you, and that is not a very good one.

Jessica: Tell me what chance that is, then.

Launcelot: Well, there is just a chance that Shylock is not truly your father.

Jessica: You may well say it is not a good one, indeed, for I would still have to bear the sin of my mother.

Launcelot: Then I fear you are lost on both accounts. If we try to avoid the one danger, we run into another, like the mariners between Scylla and Charybdis. I fear you are lost either way!

Jessica: But my husband will save me. I have become a Christian through him.

Launcelot: The more foolish is he, then, to add to the number of Christians. I am sure there are enough of us already, if we are to be able to get a livelihood. If this addition to our numbers goes on, bacon will soon become more expensive. If none are left who are forbidden to eat pork, we shall soon not have a slice of it left.

[Enter Lorenzo.]

Jessica: Here is Lorenzo. I shall let him know what you are telling me.

Lorenzo: You will be making me jealous soon, Launcelot!

Jessica: You need not be afraid of our friendship, Lorenzo. We have quarrelled now. He has just told me plainly that Heaven will show no mercy to me, because I am a Jewess. He also finds fault with you, as doing injury to your fellow citizens, for you make pork more expensive by adding to the number of those who may eat it.

Lorenzo: I really think that soon we shall appreciate only those who never speak at all, and say that the silent ones are those whose wit we enjoy most. Parrots will be the only ones who will please by their speech. Go indoors, fellow, and tell the servants to get ready for dinner.

Launcelot: They will be ready enough now, sir, for they all have appetites.

Lorenzo: Good heaven! How you catch up one's words! Tell them, then, to get the dinner ready.

Launcelot: They have done that also, sir, only we say "cover."

Lorenzo: And do you intend to "cover" also, my master?

Launcelot: Nay, sir, not I. I know my place better.

Lorenzo: What! More quibbles on everything that turns up? Are you trying to show us all your cleverness at once? Try, I beg, to absorb the meaning of simple words. Go and tell your fellow servants to lay the table and bring in the food, and we will come and eat it!

Launcelot: As for the table, signior, it shall be laid. The food shall be served. And you may come and eat it when and where you are disposed!

Lorenzo: Wonderful wisdom! How he dresses up his phrases. He has quite a stock of fine words ready for use. But there is many a one in higher ranks of life than Launcelot's who is just as foolish and no better equipped with wisdom than he, and who will let the whole sense of the subject in hand go by for the sake of playing with words and phrases. How are you, my sweet Jessica? Tell me now, dearest one, whether you like Lady Portia.

Jessica: I have no words to express my love and admiration for her. Signior Bassanio ought, indeed, to be a good man. With such a wife, he will enjoy the bliss of paradise even in this world. If he does not mean to be happy here, then he certainly does not deserve to reach happiness in the next world. If two divine beings were to make two mortals the prizes in a game, and Portia were to be one, the other would need some addition to her value, or the stakes would be unequal. There is not in this rough world another like her. She is without comparison.

Lorenzo: And just as incomparable a husband you have in me!

Jessica: Indeed! You should wait until you hear what I say on that subject.

Lorenzo: You shall tell me presently, when we have dined.

Jessica: Nay, you should hear my commendation of you while I still have an appetite for it.

Lorenzo: Let us converse about it during dinner. And then, no matter what you may say, it will all go down with the rest.

Jessica: Very well. I will show you up!

[Exit.]

ACT IV • SCENE 1

[Venice. A court of justice.]
[Enter the Duke, nobles, Antonio, Bassanio, Gratiano, Salerio and others.]

Duke: Is Antonio present?

Antonio: I am here, Your Highness.

Duke: I pity you, Antonio. Your opponent is a hard-hearted, cruel wretch, without a single grain of tenderness or sympathy in his heart.

Antonio: It has been told to me, my lord, that you have, yourself, used every endeavor to soften his severity. But, as all efforts have been in vain, and he remains obstinate, I am ready to suffer his cruelty with resignation. As the law is unable to deliver me from his malicious hatred, I am resolved to meet his utmost fury with calmness and fortitude.

Duke: Let someone go and summon Shylock to come here.

Salerio: He is standing outside, Your Highness. Here he comes.
[Enter Shylock.]

Duke: Stand aside and let him approach me. It is the general opinion, Shylock, and it is mine also, that you only intend to keep up this show of severity and hatred until it has gone as far as possible. Then, at the last moment, you intend to relent and show a kindness and pity, which will be more wonderful and amazing still, than your present appearance of unrelenting malice. And, instead of insisting on the payment of the forfeit, the flesh of this unfortunate man, you will not only let him off this payment but will generously forgive him part of his money debt to you. His losses have been so heavy and have come so thick and fast upon him lately that they have been enough to ruin even a merchant prince such as he is and to draw pity and sympathy from the most stony-hearted person, even from heathens and savages who cannot be expected to show tenderness or compassion. Everyone hopes that you will give a merciful reply to our appeal, Shylock.

Shylock: I have already informed your Majesty of my intentions and have taken an oath to exact the penalty named in the bond. If you refuse to let the law be carried out, then your city's reputation will suffer. You wish to know why I prefer a pound of flesh to a sum of money? I am not obliged to say why I do so. But suppose it is because I have a fancy for it, is that enough for you? Suppose there were vermin in my dwelling, and I chose to pay thousands of ducats to have them poisoned! Do you understand now?

Do you not know that there are many people who have a strong dislike for various objects but cannot give a sufficient reason for their dislike? Some people are sent almost frantic by the sight of a cat. Others cannot bear to see a pig. Still others loathe the scream of the bagpipe. Our feelings, when very strong, can quite overpower our reason and make it give way to what we like or dislike. As these people have no well-grounded reason to offer as to why they dislike these various objects so violently, and as they must merely make up their minds to put up with the shame of giving offence because they cannot help giving expression to the dislike they feel, I can offer you no explanation. Neither do I wish to do so, beyond the fact that I bear such a settled dislike to, and detestation of, Antonio. It influences me so greatly that I even prefer to prosecute this suit against him, although I lose the money by doing so. Have I explained clearly enough?

Bassanio: It is no excuse whatever, you hard-hearted creature, for your merciless course of action.

Shylock: I do not consider myself obliged to please you, young man, with what I say!

Bassanio: Is a man obliged to seek the death of everything he dislikes?

Shylock: If a man hates a thing intensely, would he not willingly see it die?

Bassanio: But a first offence does not rouse so fierce a hatred as that!

Shylock: Then you would give a reptile a second chance to sting!

Antonio: Remember, I beg, that you are arguing with a Jew. If you are hoping to soften his heart, you might, with equal success, take up your position on the seashore and issue orders to the ocean deeps, forbidding them to advance to their accustomed place. Or you might hope to argue with a beast of prey that has just devoured its victim, or expect that the tall pines on the hillside would be able to endure silently and without motion the onslaughts of the storm. In short, you may as soon expect to accomplish any impossibility as to be able to cause any feelings of mercy or pity to enter the hardest thing on earth, the heart of Shylock. As it is, I beg you to try no more, but, without wasting further words or time, let me have my sentence and let Shylock have what he desires!

Bassanio: I offer you, Shylock, double the amount of the debt.

Shylock: If you were to double it, and double it again three times over, I would still refuse to accept it. I want the penalty paid.

Duke: If you are so hard-hearted to others, how can you expect to be treated leniently yourself?

Shylock: I am asking for nothing but justice. Therefore, what punishment need I fear? And, as for ranting at me because I do not treat others as I would be treated myself, do you do any better? You all possess slaves, whom you employ in menial tasks as you employ your beasts of burden. You justify yourselves for this treatment of them by saying that they are yours by right of purchase. I might, if I used your own argument, say to all of you who are slave owners, "You ought to treat these people as your equals and give them their liberty. And why should they be prevented from intermarrying with your families? Why should they be forced to work for you? They ought to have the same treatment as yourselves, have as luxurious couches and as dainty fare." Your reply would be that you could treat them as you pleased, having given payment for them. My reply is the same. The pound of flesh is mine. I have given money for it, and I insist that my own property shall be given to me. If it is refused me, you will thereby make open confession that the law of Venice is a mere dead letter. I demand justice. Do you intend to give it to me?

Duke: I can dismiss this assembly by my own authority. But I will see whether the lawyer, Bellario, a man of most excellent learning and wisdom, whom I have asked to come and try this case, will arrive today.

Salerio: Your Highness, someone has just arrived from Padua with a message from Bellario. He stands outside the court.

Duke: Call him in and let me have the message.

Bassanio: Courage, my friend! Do not lose hope yet, my dear

Antonio. I will give my own flesh to the greedy Shylock and my whole body, too, before he shall have your life!

Antonio: Let me die without further ado. My honor is stained. I am bankrupt and disgraced; like a diseased creature, fit only to be taken out of the herd and slaughtered, or like the worthless fruit that drops from the tree and rots quickly! It will be a suitable task for you, my friend, to continue to live and compose the inscription for my tomb.

[Enter Nerissa, dressed like a lawyer's clerk.]

Duke: Are you the bearer of a message from Bellario of Padua?

Nerissa: Yes, Your Highness. Bellario sends his greetings.

[Presenting a letter.]

Bassanio: Why are you sharpening that knife so eagerly, Shylock?

Shylock: To be ready to cut the flesh from that man who has failed to pay his debt.

Gratiano: You sharpen it on your own soul, on the fierce hatred in your heart, rather than on the leather of your shoe. And, even then, you cannot make it as sharp as your malice. Nothing is like that, not even the keen edge of the executioner's axe. Is there no plea that will soften your heart?

Shylock: Not one that you would have wisdom enough to find!

Gratiano: Curses upon you, most villainous cur! Justice itself ought to be impeached for allowing you to live! After this I could almost believe what the ancient philosopher taught of the transmigration of souls, and think that the body of a man may sometimes be inhabited by the soul of a beast! Certainly the spirit dwelling in your breast must have formerly been that of a wolf, and when its former body was slain it took up its abode in you. All your impulses are fiendish and bloodthirsty, greedy and rapacious.

Shylock: You are only injuring your lungs, young man, by all that noise. It is mere waste of breath, unless curses could make my bond illegal. Try to get more wisdom, my young sir, or your understanding will shortly be beyond hope of improvement. All I demand is justice.

Duke: Bellario, in his letter, recommends a wise, though youthful, lawyer in his place. Is he here?

Nerissa: He is waiting nearby, my lord, until he knows whether you will allow him to undertake this case or not.

Duke: I welcome him most cordially. Let several of you go and escort him here with all politeness. While we wait for him, Bellario's letter shall be read.

Clerk: *[Reads.]* "This is to tell Your Highness that, when your letter arrived, I was very ill, but a young lawyer from Rome, called Balthasar, happened to be paying a friendly visit to me. I explained to him the case in dispute between Antonio and Shylock and told him my view of the matter. We searched many authorities on the subject, and he comes to you, armed with my opinions and instructions, to which is added his own wisdom, of which I cannot speak too highly. I begged him to undertake the case in my place, as I could not fulfil your lordship's desire. Do not let his extreme youth, I beg, prevent him from obtaining your respect and esteem. I assure Your Grace that I know of no one so young as he who is possessed of such ripe wisdom. I commend him to Your Grace, feeling confident that, when he is put to the test, his own skill will earn your praise better than any recommendations of mine."

Duke: You have heard the wise Bellario's letter. This is the young doctor he recommends, is it not?

[Enter Portia, disguised as a judge.]

I greet you, sir. You have come here at Bellario's request, I understand.

Portia: I have, sir.

Duke: We are delighted that you have come. You will now take up your position in the court. Do you understand the case before the court?

Portia: It has been thoroughly explained to me. Which of these people is Antonio, and which Shylock?

Duke: Let these two both come forward.

Portia: Are you called Shylock?

Shylock: I am.

Portia: It is a most unusual plea that you bring before the court. But it is quite legal, and the law cannot, in strictness, oppose you in it. You, Antonio, are in his power, I believe?

Antonio: Yes, it is true.

Portia: Then Shylock must have compassion on you. That is your only hope.

Shylock: And who can compel me to have mercy on him? Why should I?

58

Portia: It is the very nature of mercy that it does not act under constraint or compulsion. It is a free and gracious gift, blessing those upon whom it is shed, as the grateful showers refresh the weary earth. It has a double power, and a double blessing accompanies its exercise, benefiting both giver and receiver. Its effect is greatest when exercised by the great and powerful, and even a sovereign's power and majesty are enhanced by deeds of mercy, which shed upon him a brighter luster than his royal position can bestow. The outward symbols of his power only inspire dread. They are merely the signs of his earthly authority. But mercy's throne is in the monarch's soul, exalted far above all earthly rule. Its dominion is in the heart, and worldly considerations have no power over it. It is a divine quality, and the better an earthly ruler knows how to soften the stern decrees of justice by gracious acts of compassion, the more nearly does he approach to the divine nature of the King of Kings.

You, Shylock, ask for justice. But remember that if strict justice were to be portioned out to all, no one could escape condemnation. In our prayers, we ask that compassion may be shown to us. We ought to learn from that very petition to show pity to others. My object in speaking thus is to try to persuade you to forgo your legal rights. For, if you insist upon them, the impartial judges of this court will have no choice but to decide the case in your favor and against Antonio.

Shylock: I am quite ready to take the consequences of my own act. I demand justice and the carrying out of the agreement.

Portia: Can Antonio not pay the debt?

Bassanio: Yes, here it is. I offer double the amount. If the Jew thinks that too little, I pledge myself to pay the amount 10 times over, on penalty of losing my own life. If he refuses this, then it will be plainly seen that this suit is only pushed forward from pure spite and ill will. And let me beg of you, sir, to stretch the law a little aside for once. The great good you will do will far outweigh the slight inaccuracy necessary to obtain it, and prevent this fiendish Jew from succeeding in his cruel design.

Portia: That cannot be done. No authority is powerful enough to set aside the laws of the land. If it were done once, it would furnish an example for future imitation and would probably lead to the introduction of many grave abuses. It is therefore impossible to do as you wish.

Shylock: A marvellous young judge, as wise as Daniel! How I respect you, wise youth!

Portia: Let me see the agreement, I beg.

Shylock: This is it, honorable sir.

Portia: Think again, Jew. You are offered the money many times over.

Shylock: I have vowed, I have sworn, that I will have the forfeit. Do you think I can break my oath? Not for all the state!

Portia: Well, then, the agreement has been broken, and the penalty must be paid. This gives Shylock the legal right to a pound of flesh, cut from Antonio's breast. Shylock, have pity and let me destroy the agreement.

Shylock: Yes, when it has been fulfilled, according to what is written in it. You show plainly, by your wise explanation and just decision, that your knowledge of the law is very sound. I therefore demand that the law, which you uphold so worthily, be put in operation and that the sentence be pronounced. I vow most solemnly that no persuasions of any kind can make me change my mind. I take my stand on the agreement.

Antonio: With all my heart, I beg that the sentence may be pronounced at once.

Portia: This, then, is the sentence. You must be ready to pay the penalty.

Shylock: O worthy judge! Most honorable youth!

Portia: The provisions of the law are clearly applicable to this case, as it stands here in the agreement.

Shylock: You are right, O learned and honorable judge! How much riper is your wisdom than your youthful appearance would lead one to expect!

Portia: You must therefore, Antonio, expose your breast to the knife.

Shylock: Yes, it is so written down. The exact words are "Close to his heart," are they not, most worthy sir?

Portia: You are quite right. Have you the scales ready, to see that you get the just weight?

Shylock: Yes, here they are.

Portia: Let a doctor be at hand, Shylock, at your expense, so that he may close Antonio's wound and perhaps prevent him from losing his life.

Shylock: Is that mentioned in the agreement?

Portia: No, it is not specially mentioned, but that does not matter. It is only right that you should do so, out of kindness.

Shylock: I do not see it written here. It is not in the agreement.

Portia: Do you wish to say anything, Antonio?

Antonio: I have little to say. I have prepared myself for death and fortified my spirit to meet it with courage. Bassanio, adieu, let me take your hand in mine, and do not sorrow too deeply that this has happened to me for your sake. Indeed, fate has dealt less harshly with me than with many others. It generally happens that, when misfortune overtakes a man, he lives to see the ruin that has come upon him, and to endure an old age of hardships and sufferings. But I am escaping these prolonged sorrows by an early death. Bear my greetings to your noble lady and tell her the story of my death. Tell her also of my true and faithful friendship for you and say all the good you can about me when I am dead. Then, when you have told her all, let her decide whether her husband had or had not a true and loyal friend. If only I know that you will grieve for my death because of your love for me, then I shall not grieve that I am doing this for your sake. I pay the penalty freely. Should Shylock's knife penetrate far enough, I shall, shortly, pay it with my heart's blood.

Bassanio: I have a wife, Antonio, whom I love as dearly as my own life. But I rate your life above my own, above my beloved wife and above everything else on earth, and I would give up all, if by so doing I could persuade this fiend to spare your life.

Portia: If your wife were within hearing, she would not be very grateful to you for your offer.

Gratiano: I also am married, and I swear I love my wife. But I could almost wish she were dead, so that she might beg someone in paradise to influence the mind of this fiend.

Nerissa: You may be thankful that you do not utter this wish in her hearing, or there would certainly be a quarrel between you.

Shylock: *[Aside.]* So that is all that Christian husbands think of their wives. I wish that any of the most villainous of Jews had married my daughter, rather than one of these Nazarenes.

[Aloud.] Come! The time is being wasted. Let the sentence be carried out, I pray.

Portia: You are entitled to a pound of Antonio's flesh. It is yours by law, and the court gives it to you.

Shylock: O honest judge!

Portia: And this flesh must be taken from his breast. The court gives it to you; it is legally yours.

Shylock: O wise and honorable judge! A just decision! Get ready, Antonio!

Portia: Wait a moment. I have more to say. In this agreement, there is no mention whatever of any blood. It is clearly written here — "a pound of flesh." You are allowed to take the forfeited pound of flesh. It is your right, according to the agreement. But if, in the process of obtaining the flesh, you cause the blood of a Christian citizen to be shed, then all your wealth and possessions are forfeited to the government, for so it is stated in the Venetian law.

Gratiano: O honorable judge! Notice well, Shylock. A most wise judge!

Shylock: Is there really such a law?

Portia: It shall be shown to you. You shall see that you get justice, as you plead so insistently for it. And it may be that the justice will be more strict than you will altogether wish for.

Gratiano: O most wise judge! Notice, Shylock. A shrewd and sagacious judge!

Shylock: I will accept the offer, then, that was made at first. I will release the Nazarene from his bond on payment of three times the amount of the debt.

Bassanio: Here! Take the amount.

Portia: Gently! Shylock shall have the justice he asks for, to the fullest extent. There is no hurry. Wait a little! He shall have what was named in the bond. No more.

Gratiano: Now, Shylock! Is he not a wise and prudent judge!

Portia: You may therefore take the forfeit, but be careful that you do not spill a single drop of blood or sever a smaller or larger amount than one exact pound. Should it weigh lighter or heavier by the merest fraction, should the balance move no more than a hair's width, you place yourself under sentence of death, and your possessions are forfeited to the state.

Gratiano: A judge with the wisdom of Daniel, Shylock! A new Daniel, educated and prudent! Now you are fairly caught, you unbeliever!

Portia: Well, Shylock, why do you hesitate? Take your pound of flesh!

Shylock: Let me have the original amount I lent, and I will leave the court.

Bassanio: Take it. It is here waiting for you.

Portia: He has already said, in front of all the people present, that he would not have it. All he wanted was justice and the payment of the penalty, and those he shall have.

Gratiano: I say it again, a modern Daniel is here! Many thanks, Shylock, for telling me that expressive phrase.

Shylock: Am I not even to have the money I lent?

Portia: You will only be given what was named in the bond, and on your own head be the consequences of taking it!

Shylock: Let him keep it, then, and may Satan give him the benefit of it. I will wait for no further arguments!

Portia: Wait a moment, Shylock. You have put yourself into the power of the law in yet another way. One of the statutes declares that if a foreigner should conspire against any of the citizens of Venice and should try to achieve his death, either directly or by any devious means, then the person whom he has plotted against is entitled to half his wealth. The rest is to be handed over to the government's private treasury, and the life of the plotter himself depends solely on the will of the Duke. Now you, Shylock, have placed yourself in this awkward position. For it has been openly shown that it was the death of Antonio you wished for, and you endeavored to bring that about by every means in your power. You, therefore, have brought upon yourself the punishment of which I have already spoken. Your only hope lies in the Duke's mercy. Get on your knees at once, and plead for pardon.

Gratiano: Ask him to give you permission to go and hang yourself! But even that is out of your power now, for you have absolutely nothing left, since all your possessions are confiscated. So even the rope must be provided by the state.

Duke: I give you your life, Shylock, before you have petitioned for it, in order to show you that our hearts are not so vengeful as yours. As for half your riches, they now belong to the merchant you have plotted against. The rest is forfeited to the government. However, if you show your repentance, the state may impose merely a fine instead of taking the full amount.

Portia: Yes, from the portion that comes to the state, not from Antonio's half.

Shylock: Oh! What is the use of sparing my life? You may as well take that also, seeing that you have taken away my means of subsistence. How can I live when you are reducing me to being a beggar?

Portia: Can you forgive him, Antonio, and show him any kindness?

Gratiano: Give him a rope, free. That is all he should have, by Heaven!

Antonio: I would be very glad if the Duke would be gracious enough to forgive him the forfeiture of the half of his wealth that comes to the state, and if he will also allow me to use the portion that I receive to the best advantage for the present, and, on the death of the Jew, to turn it over to Lorenzo, to whom Jessica, Shylock's daughter, has recently been married. But there are two conditions to be made: one is that, in return for this forgiveness, he shall at once embrace the Christian faith, and the other that now, in front of this court, he shall sign a deed leaving all his possessions at his death to Jessica and her husband.

Duke: I decree that he must fulfil these conditions, or otherwise I will withdraw the forgiveness that I have just extended to him.

Portia: Does this satisfy you, Shylock? What answer do you return to the Duke?

Shylock: I agree.

Portia: Then let the clerk prepare the document.

Shylock: I beg you to allow me to depart. I am ill. I will add my signature to the paper if it is brought to me later.

Duke: Go, then, but see that you fulfil your promise.

Gratiano: When you are baptized into the Christian faith, two sponsors will stand for you. But, if it had lain in my power to pronounce the sentence, it would have been 12 jurymen, who would have sentenced you to be hanged, not baptized!

[Exit Shylock.]

Duke: I beg that you will dine with me, sir.

Portia: Pardon me, my lord. I beg you most kindly to excuse me, for I must set out on my return to Padua at once.

Duke: I regret that you have no time to remain longer. Antonio, in my opinion, you are greatly indebted to this gentleman, and you will, no doubt, reward him as he deserves.

[Exit Duke and his followers.]

Bassanio: Honored signior, my dear Antonio and I have been delivered from a most terrible position today by your skill and learning. We therefore ask you to accept, as a small return for your trouble, the sum that was due to Shylock.

Antonio: Even this will not repay our obligation to you. If we can ever be of any service to you, we shall consider it a favor if you will command us.

Portia: One who is well pleased with his work is sufficiently rewarded. I am well pleased that I have been the means of liberating you from the power of the Jew, and I consider that a sufficient reward. I have never thought of any other payment than the pleasure of doing a good action. I shall be happy to renew our acquaintance later. I will now say farewell, with many good wishes for your welfare.

Bassanio: Worthy signior, I really must ask you to accept something as a token of our gratitude. If you will not take it as payment for your skill, let it be a gift, a token of our friendship. Please do not refuse me this, and, I beg you, forgive my persistence.

Portia: You urge me so strongly, that I really cannot refuse. *[To Antonio.]* As a token of our friendship, I will accept the gloves that you are carrying, and *[To Bassanio.]* the ring that you are wearing. Nay, sir, do not make any objections. I do not ask anything further, and, surely, the professions of love and gratitude you have just made will not allow you to refuse me.

Bassanio: Indeed, worthy signior, this ring is far from valuable. I really could not think of allowing you to accept so small a gift.

Portia: I do not wish for anything except the ring, and I really feel that I would like to possess that.

Bassanio: I do not hesitate merely because of the worth of the ring. I am influenced by other considerations. I will send a proclamation throughout the whole city and discover the most valuable ring in it to present to you. But I beg you to forgive me if I refuse this one.

Portia: You show plainly, sir, that you make promises very freely. I asked for nothing until you urged me, and now you will make me learn what kind of reply is given to those who ask.

Bassanio: My dear sir, my wife presented this ring to me, and I swore to her that I would never part with it!

Portia: Many a man who does not wish to give a present gives that as his reason for refusing. If your lady is a sensible person and understands what I have done to deserve a gift from you, she will soon relent and moderate her displeasure when you tell her I have her ring. However, farewell!

[Exit Portia and Nerissa.]

Antonio: My dear Bassanio, do not refuse him the ring. Let the promise you made to your wife be outweighed, on this occasion, by his merits and by the love you bear me.

Bassanio: Gratiano, hasten, and see whether you can reach him before he departs. Take the ring to him, and also an invitation to Antonio's house. See if you can convince him to come back with you. Go quickly! Lose no time. *[Exit Gratiano.]* Come, Antonio, we will proceed to your house at once and be ready to hasten in the morning to Belmont. Let us go!

[Exit.]

ACT IV • SCENE 2

[A street.]
[Enter Portia and Nerissa.]

Portia: Ask someone to direct you to Shylock's house, then deliver this paper to him for his signature. After that, we will set out for Belmont, and reach it the day before Signior Bassanio and your husband arrive. Lorenzo will be greatly delighted to receive this document.

[Enter Gratiano.]

Gratiano: Noble signior, I am happy to have overtaken you. After further consideration, Signior Bassanio asks you to accept the ring and also asks you to dine with him.

Portia: Please tell him I will take his gift with pleasure and gratitude, but it is impossible for me to dine with him. And now, I beg you, kindly direct my boy to the dwelling of the Jew.

Gratiano: I will show him with pleasure.

Nerissa: May I have a word with you, sir? *[Aside to Portia.]* I shall try to obtain his ring also, though he vowed never to part with it.

Portia: *[Aside to Nerissa.]* I expect you will succeed. And then, what vows they will make to us that they have bestowed their rings upon men as a gift. But we shall contradict them and swear just as strongly that they are deceiving us. *[Aloud.]* Come, hasten! You remember where I am to wait for you.

Nerissa: Kind signior, will you direct me to the house of Shylock?

[Exit.]

ACT V •SCENE 1

[Belmont. Avenue to Portia's house.]
[Enter Lorenzo and Jessica.]

Lorenzo: How brilliant the moon's rays are tonight! They shone as brilliantly, long ages ago, on a still, calm evening in Troy. The gentle breeze breathed softly through the trees, which silently received its sweet caressing. Within the besieged city, the youthful warrior prince climbed to the outward ramparts and looked with longing eyes toward the camp of the besiegers, where his beloved one lay sleeping.

Jessica: They shone as brilliantly that night when Thisbe, with a heart throbbing with fear, came daintily stepping over the dewy grass. The bright rays showed her the shadow of the terrible beast of prey, and, warned in time, she fled to safety.

Lorenzo: It was as fair a night when the lovely queen of Carthage, bearing the emblem of forsaken love, stood on the beach watching the ships of Aeneas leave her shores, stretching her arms toward him in a vain appeal for his return.

Jessica: On as fair a night as this, Medea went forth to obtain the magic herbs with which to work her spells, by means of which she gave the aged Aeson the gift of renewed youth.

Lorenzo: On just so bright an evening as this did Shylock's sweet daughter leave her rich old father to run away with a penniless husband from the city and come to Belmont.

Jessica: And on just so bright a night, her lover swore to her many vows of love. And he won her heart with promises of constancy and affection, and there was not a word of truth in one of them!

Lorenzo: And on as bright a night as this, the lovely little Jewess mocked and spoke evil of her husband, and he pardoned it all!

Jessica: I could beat you in offering instances of the night, if we only had a little longer time to ourselves. But there are footsteps approaching.

[Enter Stephano.]

Lorenzo: Who is this approaching with such haste, through the still evening air?

Stephano: A friend.

Lorenzo: Who are you, then? And what is your name?

Stephano: I am called Stephano, and I come to tell you that Portia will arrive at Belmont before morning. She is making her way here past the shrines of sacred emblems, where she is offering her prayers for blessings on her wedded life.

Lorenzo: Has she any companion?

Stephano: A pious monk is with her, and her gentlewoman, Nerissa. Has my lord Bassanio reached home?

Lorenzo: Not yet, nor have we had any news concerning him. Come, Jessica, let us go into the house and be ready to greet our lady with suitable form and ceremony.

[Enter Launcelot.]

Launcelot: Hallo! Ta-ra-ra! Tarantara!

Lorenzo: Who is there?

Launcelot: Have you seen master Lorenzo? Ta-ra-ra!

Lorenzo: Stop shouting, fellow, here I am!

Launcelot: Ta-ra-ra! Where are you?

Lorenzo: Here!

Launcelot: A messenger has just arrived with the welcome tidings that my lord Bassanio will arrive here before break of day.

[Exit.]

Lorenzo: Dear one, let us go and await their arrival within the house. Wait! That is not necessary, there is no reason that we should not wait out here. You, Stephano, please be good enough to go and announce to the servants that Portia will soon arrive, and then let the musicians bring their instruments and perform outside. *[Exit Stephano.]* How softly the rays of moonlight fall upon this grassy slope! Let us seat ourselves here and listen, while the sweet music steals upon the air. Its melodious tones are heard most suitably in the hush of night. Be seated here, beloved! See, how all the heavenly expanse above us is studded with glittering gems! And every radiant sphere you see is continually singing such sweet music as the angels hear, its ordered movements in company with its shining fellows creating the harmonies of the spheres. And just such music do our everliving spirits produce. But, as long as we must dwell in these mortal bodies, wrapped up in these perishable garments of clay, its heavenly tones are inaudible to our ears.

[Enter musicians.]

Now, sound your sweetest notes, until their tones reach

the sleeping moon goddess, and she shall arouse herself to hear. And let your harmonies ring forth upon the night until they reach Portia travelling homeward and bring her back to the accompaniment of your melodies.

[Music.]

Jessica: When I listen to beautiful music, I always feel sad.

Lorenzo: That is because it touches your heart. Your spirit responds to the beautiful tones. Even savage and untamed beasts or a number of wild, unbroken young horses rushing madly over the plains, prancing wildly about with clamorous cries, so full are they of energy and fierce strength, come quickly to a halt and remain quietly listening, gazing calmly with eyes that recently were so fierce, if they hear the tones of a bugle ring out, or if they are within hearing of any sweet melody being played. So powerful is the influence of music over even the brute creation. Thus it is written in the ancient legends that Orpheus could sway all things by the power of his lute's music. Trees waved, stones moved and rivers followed where he walked. For there is surely nothing in the world so insensible to soft influences, so fierce and unyielding, that it does not, even for a passing moment, yield to the power of music. If there is any human creature whose spirit is untouched by the sweet influence of music or whose soul is incapable of responding to the beauty of sweet harmonies, his thoughts are low and earthly, his spirit has no spark of brighter feelings, and his emotions are sordid, base and covetous, incapable of anything but underhanded plots and deceptions. Never rely on the goodness of such a man! Now, let us listen to the melody.

[Enter Portia and Nerissa.]

Portia: Those bright rays are from a light within my house. How far they shine out into the night. Just so does the light of a kind action pierce the darkness of the surrounding wickedness on the earth.

Nerissa: But the rays of the candle are outshone by those of the moon.

Portia: Yes. In that we see that the effect of small things is overshadowed by the fame of greater ones. In the absence of the sovereign, the viceroy holds as brilliant a state and looks to all beholders as glorious as his master. But, when the king himself appears, the other's glories vanish. He humbles himself and is lost sight of in the brightness of the sovereign's magnificence, as a little stream loses itself in the mighty ocean. But listen! I hear music!

Nerissa: They are your own musicians who are playing.

Portia: We appreciate things much better, I find, when we have leisure to pay regard to them. The music appears to be much more pleasing when heard by night.

Nerissa: That is because of the stillness in which it is heard. There are no other sounds to distract the attention from its beauty.

Portia: True, for the sweetest note of the lark makes no more impression on our spirits than the hoarse voice of the crow if we are paying no attention to either of them. Even the sweetest of all bird minstrels, the nightingale, would not be appreciated more than the twittering wren if she sang her lovely melodies during the busy hours of daylight, when foolish, discordant sounds everywhere fill the air. How often is the true value of a thing discovered and appreciated by the mere fact of its having been seen or heard at the most suitable time! But silence! Diana rests on the mountaintop with the sleeping shepherd lad. Disturb her not!

[Music ceases.]

Lorenzo: I am very greatly mistaken if that is not Portia speaking.

Portia: He recognizes me by my note, as a blind man can tell a cuckoo when he hears it.

Lorenzo: We are made happy by your return, sweet lady.

Portia: Our time has been spent in prayers on behalf of our husbands, and we trust that they have prospered the better on account of our petitions. Have they arrived yet from Venice?

Lorenzo: No, lady, they are not here. But a courier has arrived in advance to announce their speedy arrival.

Portia: Nerissa, go and tell my attendants within the house that they are not to speak of our absence or make any allusion to it, and you, Lorenzo and Jessica, do not do so either!

[A trumpet sounds.]

Lorenzo: Signior Bassanio is near. That bugle note announced his coming. But have no fear, we will not betray your secret.

Portia: This night appears to be only a feebler copy of the day. It is not quite so brightly colored, but that is all. The day, itself, is often just so dim when clouds obscure the sun.

[Enter Bassanio, Antonio, Gratiano and their followers.]

Bassanio: If you, sweet lady, were to come forth at night after the sun has left us, we would still have day, even while the sun is lighting up the opposite side of the globe.

Portia: Willingly would I bestow light, but most unwillingly would I behave lightly. Light behavior causes heavy hearts, and never shall my husband be heavy-hearted on my account. However, we will leave these matters to God. Meantime, we are happy in your return.

Bassanio: Lady, many thanks. And now, greet my dear friend, Antonio, to whom I owe so much, and bid him welcome to our house.

Portia: It is only right that you should consider yourself greatly indebted to him, for I am told that he was greatly in debt to another for your sake.

Antonio: Not so deeply that I have not been happily released.

Portia: I am most happy to see you here, Signior Antonio, but I trust to show you the warmth of my welcome in a more substantial manner. Therefore, I will say no more in mere words.

Gratiano: *[To Nerissa.]* I vow by the light of the moon above us that you are accusing me unjustly! Really and truly, it was the lawyer's young clerk to whom I gave it. I wish the one I gave it to were dead, as it has displeased you so much, dearest.

Portia: What do I hear? Wrangling already? What is it all about?

Gratiano: A golden circlet, a worthless ring that Nerissa bestowed upon me, with a rhyming inscription on it, such as the manufacturers engrave on an ordinary knife — "Be loving and faithful."

Nerissa: What does the worth of the ring, or the inscription, matter? When I gave it to you, you solemnly vowed that you would never part with it during life. And that after death, it would rest in the tomb with you. Even if you did not care sufficiently to keep it for my sake, for the sake of not breaking your earnest vow, you should have had more regard for it and for your promise. Bestowed it on a young clerk, indeed! I declare before Heaven that the clerk who got it will never own a beard.

Gratiano: Yes, he will, unless he die before he has grown to manhood.

Nerissa: Yes, no doubt he will, if a woman ever grow to manhood.

Gratiano: I swear by my right hand, it was a boy I gave it to — a little, short youth no taller than you are. He was clerk to the young lawyer and talked, coaxed and entreated me to give him the ring in payment for his services, until I could not be so hard-hearted as to refuse him any longer.

Portia: I must say that it is my candid opinion that it was very wrong of you to give away so readily the first present your wife had given you. And it had also been accompanied by eager vows when it was placed upon your hand and so was tightly bound upon your body with vows of faithfulness. I also bestowed a ring upon the man who loves me, and who stands here before us. He vowed that he would never let it leave his finger. I am willing to take an oath on his behalf that he would not part with it nor give it away, though he were offered all the riches of the universe. Honestly, Gratiano, you have given Nerissa a very just ground of complaint. If it were me, I would be really angry.

Bassanio: *[Aside.]* I think the best thing I can do is to cut off the hand that wore the ring, and vow that the ring was taken from me by force, and that I was wounded in trying to prevent it.

Gratiano: But Signior Bassanio did part with his ring. He gave it to the lawyer, who had asked for it, and who really merited a reward. When his clerk saw that, the youth, who was a painstaking writer, asked me to give him mine. We offered them a payment in money instead, but no other gift except our rings would satisfy them.

Portia: Which of your rings did you give the lawyer, Bassanio? I trust it was not the one I gave you.

Bassanio: If I were inclined to make my offence worse by adding falsehood to it, I might swear it was not so. But here I show you my hand. You perceive the ring is no longer there.

Portia: And just so there is no longer any trust to be placed on your word, just so empty is your bosom of honesty. I vow that you shall never call me wife until you can show me the ring again.

Nerissa: Nor shall you, Gratiano, before you show me mine once more.

Bassanio: Dearest lady, if you had been acquainted with the one who received the ring, and if you knew the man for whose sake I gave it, if you would but think what good reason I had for bestowing it, and could imagine how reluctantly I parted with it when I found that in no other way could I satisfy him, I think you would be less angry.

Portia: If you had been acquainted with the special qualities possessed by the ring, and if you knew half the virtues of the woman who bestowed it on you or had considered how you were honor bound to keep it as you had vowed, you would never have given it away. If you had chosen to oppose his request with any earnestness whatever, surely he would not have been so persistent or so wanting in good feeling as to press you for a thing which you held almost sacred? I am forced to learn from Nerissa what has happened. On my life, you have given it to a woman!

Bassanio: I swear by all that is most sacred to me, lady, that I never gave it to a woman but to a most learned and courteous lawyer. He would not accept any fee, even when I offered him the whole sum of money due to the Jew. All he asked for was the ring. I refused to bestow it upon him, although he was the very one who had saved Antonio's life, and he left the court greatly disappointed. Dear lady, how could I appear so ungrateful? I was overwhelmed with feelings of shame at my apparent thanklessness to one who had just rendered us such an important service. Ordinary politeness advised me to do whatever he might ask. I could not allow my reputation to be so tarnished. I was obliged to let a messenger follow him with the ring he so much wished for. Dearest Portia, forgive me. By the stars above us I swear that, if you had been present, you would have pleaded with me to let him have it.

Portia: I hope for your sake that that lawyer will keep away from your home, for I shall follow your example. You have bestowed on him the gem that I prized so highly because he

asked for it. Therefore, I shall consider that I am entitled also to bestow on him anything I possess.

Nerissa: And I shall refuse nothing that his clerk asks for. Therefore, have a care that you do not leave me unguarded.

Gratiano: Give him what you please, but I warn you that, if I catch him, I shall spoil his fine handwriting for him.

Antonio: I am truly grieved to be the cause of all this wrangling.

Portia: Do not let that trouble you, Signior Antonio. We are glad to see you here, in spite of this.

Bassanio: Pardon me, dear lady, that I was compelled to displease you in this. I make a vow, with all these friends as witnesses, and swear to you, by your two lovely eyes that reflect my image —

Portia: Hear what he says! He sees himself in each of my eyes. Therefore, he sees himself double. Truly, a most appropriate oath, to vow by his double-dealing self!

Bassanio: Only listen, lady. Forgive me this one offence, and I vow by my soul, that never again will you have cause to reproach me with a broken promise.

Antonio: Once already I have been security for the welfare of your husband. And, had it not been for the worthy doctor to whom Bassanio gave your ring, my pledge would have been forfeited. Yet, so sure am I of your husband's faithfulness that I would not fear to be his security again, offering my soul as the pledge this time, and swear that never again will Bassanio knowingly break his word to you.

Portia: I accept your offer, and you shall be guarantee for his faith. Here is a ring. Give it to him and tell him to take better care of it than he did of the last one.

Antonio: Signior Bassanio, take this ring and take an oath that you will never part with it.

Bassanio: Powers above! This is the ring I gave to the lawyer!

Portia: You seem overwhelmed with astonishment. But read this letter when you have time; it will explain. Bellario of Padua sends it to you. You will see in it that the lawyer was Portia, herself, and the young clerk, Nerissa. Lorenzo can testify that we started on our journey immediately after you, and we have only just returned. In fact, I have not even been within my doors yet. Once more I bid you welcome, Signior Antonio. I have unexpected good tidings for you, also. Open your letter quickly and read it. It will inform you of a stroke of good fortune. Three of your vessels have unexpectedly reached their destination, with all their rich cargo intact. I shall not tell you how curiously I happened to obtain the letter.

Antonio: Lady, you have rendered me speechless.

Bassanio: Were you really the lawyer, and I never recognized you?

Gratiano: Were you really the doctor's clerk, and I did not know you?

Antonio: Dear madam, your hand has restored not only my life but my means of living. This letter tells me that, without doubt, my vessels have arrived safely.

Portia: Now, Lorenzo, it is your turn. Nerissa has some welcome news for you also.

Nerissa: Yes, and I shall make no charge for it. Here, Lorenzo, I present a letter to you from the wealthy Shylock, bestowing all his riches and possessions upon you and Jessica at his death.

Lorenzo: Dear ladies, your hands scatter blessings wherever you go and provide food for the hungry.

Portia: The day is almost dawning, yet we have not had time to explain all to your satisfaction. Come indoors, and ask all that you wish. We will give you full and complete answers to all your questions.

Gratiano: I can only say that my chief care for the rest of my life will be to guard my wife's ring and never to part with it.

[Exit.]